DATE DUE		

900

HIS   History /

Native North Americans
History

BROWN
BEAR
BOOKS

Published by Brown Bear Books Limited

An imprint of:
The Brown Reference Group Ltd
68 Topstone Road
Redding
Connecticut 06896
USA
www.brownreference.com

© 2009 The Brown Reference Group Ltd

ISBN: 978-1-933-834-82-5

Editorial Director: Lindsey Lowe
Senior Managing Editor: Tim Cooke
Managing Editor: Laura Durman
Editors: Amy Bauman and Laura Durman
Designer: Rob Norridge
Picture Researcher: Rachel Tisdale

Library of Congress Cataloging-in-Publication Data available upon request

Picture Credits

Contents

Introduction

Native North Americans forms part of the Curriculum Connections project. The six volumes of the set cover all aspects of the history and culture of native peoples in what are now the United States and Canada. Each volume covers a particular aspect of Native American life: Peoples of the East, Southeast, and Plains; Peoples of the Southwest, West, and North; Arts, Society, and Religion; History; Personalities and Places; and Warfare, Economy, and Technology.

About this set

Each volume in *Native North Americans* features a series of articles arranged in A–Z order. The articles are all listed in the contents pages of each book, and can also be located through the indexes.

Each illustrated article provides a concise but accurate summary of its subject, accompanied where relevant by informative maps. Articles about major tribes are each accompanied by a fact file that provides a summary of essential information.

Within each article, two key aids to learning are located in sidebars in the margins of each page:

Curriculum Context sidebars indicate that a subject has particular relevance to state and national American history guidelines and curricula. They highlight essential information or suggest useful ways for students to include a subject in their studies.

Glossary sidebars define key words within the text.

At the end of the book, a summary Glossary lists the key terms defined in the volume. There is also a list of further print and Web-based resources and a full volume index.

About this book

Native peoples had already inhabited North America for thousands of years before Europeans arrived at the end of the 15th century. Much of this early history was unrecorded, however, and its interpretation relies on archaeological evidence. Most of the articles in this book deal with events since the European arrival, which are far better understood. The Europeans encountered a wide range of peoples, from the mighty Aztec empire in what is now central Mexico to scattered bands of hunters and farmers who lived along the Missouri.

Since the arrival of Europeans, much of Native American history has been the history of how tribal societies interacted with the newcomers. Initial contact was often friendly: the story is well known of how Native Americans saved the settlers at Jamestown on the first Thanksgiving, and European traders were eager to deal with native fur trappers. As North America became a battleground in Europe's colonial struggles, however, so native peoples became involved either as allies of the competing powers or indirectly, finding their traditional territory and lifestyle under threat from European expansion.

After the American Revolution, the story of most Native American groups has been one of struggle, resistance, and eventual defeat. By the end of the 19th century resistance was at an effective end and virtually all native groups had been consigned to reservations, sometimes thousands of miles from their original homeland. In the late 20th century, however, a campaign for improved civil rights and self-government for tribal lands has led to an improvement in the standard of life of some tribes, although others still suffer from harsh poverty and discrimination.

Allotment Act

The Allotment Act, which is the common name for the Dawes Severalty Act, was passed by the U.S. government and became law in February 1887. The act had three aims—to bring about an end to the Native American reservation system, to encourage private land ownership, and to make Native Americans full U.S. citizens.

Curriculum Context

Curricula may ask students to study federal Indian policy after the Civil War and evaluate its legacy and effects on tribal identity and land ownership.

The law allowed U.S. officials to survey reservation lands. The aim of these surveys was to lay the foundations for the dividing up of the reservations into plots of land of varying sizes, which would then be settled by individual Native Americans. Previously, reservations had belonged to a tribe, not to an individual, and were used as a communal resource.

Under the Allotment Act, land was to be owned privately. The act stated that each Native American family would be entitled to a plot of 160 acres (64 ha) for growing crops; single adults over 18 would be eligible to receive a plot of half the size, while dependent minors (those under 18 years of age) would be offered 40 acres (16 ha). If the land was to be used for livestock, the grants would be doubled. Those Native Americans who accepted the plots automatically became U.S. citizens

Selling reservation land

By implementing the Allotment Act, the government was riding roughshod over all previous individual treaties signed by Native Americans. Many of these treaties had guaranteed Native Americans the right to their reservation lands forever. However, the U.S. government believed that owning and farming land would help Native Americans integrate into mainstream white American life.

Roughshod

Roughly; without thought or carefulness.

Under the act, Native Americans were forbidden from either selling or renting out their land for a period of 25 years. And any reservation lands that were unoccupied once the Native Americans had settled on their government-designated plots could be sold. This loophole was exploited by many land-hungry whites. Further, the authorities did not take into account that many Native American cultures were still based on hunting, not farming.

Repealing the act

The Allotment Act was in force from 1887 to 1934. During that time land held by Native Americans dropped from an estimated 140 million acres (57 million ha) to a little less than 50 million acres (20 million ha). Many tribes attempted to prevent the Allotment Act from being enforced, some arguing that reservation land could not be sold without the agreement of a majority of the tribe involved. The tribes were rarely successful in preventing the government from imposing a sale.

The Allotment Act was highly controversial and unpopular. In June 1934 the U.S. government enacted the Indian Reorganization Act, also known as the Wheeler–Howard Act. This stopped the allocation of allotments but also went further. Tribes were allowed to purchase extra land, Native American businesses were offered loans, and individual Native Americans were given preference in the civil service. The act also gave tribes the right to draw up their own constitutions as a basis of Native American self-government.

Curriculum Context

Many curricula ask students to analyze political aspects of the conflict between Native Americans and the U.S. government over land ownership.

Allocation

The distribution or sharing out of something.

The American Civil War

By the time of the Civil War (1861–1865) most Native Americans lived west of the Mississippi River. Many of them believed that the war was a white person's affair and no business of theirs. They were partly right. All of the major battles of the war took place east of the Mississippi River, and most of the soldiers on both sides were white, although by 1865 about 10 percent of the Union forces were African Americans.

Curriculum Context

Curricula may ask students to analyze Native American involvement in the Civil War and evaluate the consequences of that involvement on their societies.

Five Civilized Tribes

The Cherokee, Chickasaw, Choctaw, Creek, and Seminole were given this name by European settlers because their lives were organized in a way that reminded the colonists of their own.

In 1861 many Native Americans whose reservations were close to the border between the Union (the North) and the Confederacy (the South) were living peacefully with white settlers. This was especially true in the officially designated Indian Territory (the modern state of Oklahoma). However, each side in the Civil War was desperate to build up its military forces and tried to persuade Native Americans to join in the fighting. In the Indian Territory, it was initially difficult for most Native Americans to avoid having to choose between the North and the South.

The Civil War had only an indirect effect on Native Americans who lived in parts of the Southwest and the Plains. In these areas there had been various clashes between white settlers and Native Americans from the 1850s onward. During the Civil War, a growing number of whites passed through and even settled in these areas. This merely served to intensify the fighting between Native Americans and white settlers.

War in Indian Territory

Since the mid-18th century, the Five Civilized Tribes had dominated the Indian Territory, although many other groups were also living there. The territory was a focus for unrest and resentment, since most tribes living there had been displaced from their original homelands.

At the beginning of the Civil War, the Indian Territory was bordered to the south and east by the Confederate states of Texas and Arkansas. But to the north and northeast lay Kansas and Missouri, Union territories that were hotly disputed by the Union and the Confederacy. The Indian Territory was therefore cut off from the main parts of the Union.

Within months of the start of fighting, the few Union garrisons stationed in the Indian Territory pulled out and went east. This also meant that the money paid from the U.S. government to help run the Native American schools and the local institutions was cut off. All of the U.S. government agents responsible for dealings with the Native Americans in the Indian Territory chose to join the Confederacy and, together with representatives from Arkansas and Texas, tried to

Native Americans fought in several battles inside, and outside, the Indian Territory during the Civil War.

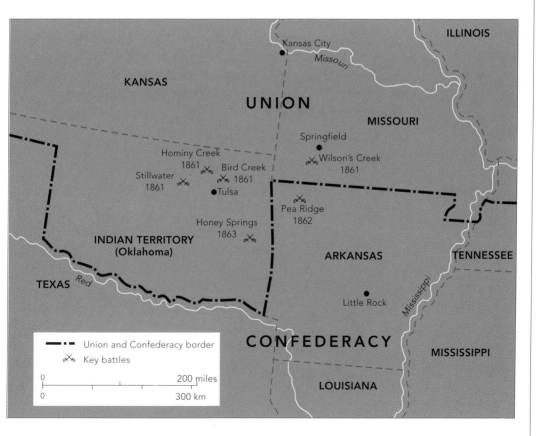

persuade the Native Americans to join the Confederate cause. Various Native Americans agreed and made treaties with the South in July 1861.

Of the Five Civilized Tribes, most of the Choctaw and Chickasaw people chose to join the South, but the Cherokee, Creek, and Seminole were divided. Many thought that since they had made a treaty with the U.S. government, they should support the Union. This group was led by John Ross, a Cherokee chief of part-Scottish ancestry. Other leaders such as Stand Watie, also a Cherokee, decided that the Union had abandoned the Native Americans and that it would be best to make a new deal with the Confederacy.

Choosing sides

Stand Watie raised a regiment of Native American soldiers to fight on the Confederate side. In August 1861 that regiment played an important part in the Confederacy's victory at the Battle of Wilson's Creek in Missouri.

After this, John Ross decided that it was better for his people to be united on one side in the war. The Confederates, under the leadership of Stand Watie, who had been made a general, finally surrendered. At the end of the Civil War, Watie was the last of all the Confederate generals to surrender.

After the Civil War

For the Indian Territory, the Civil War had devastating effects, both short- and long-term. Raids and counter-raids had destroyed many homes, crops, and farm animals, forcing some Native Americans in the area to completely rebuild their lives.

In addition to repairing all this damage, the Native Americans in the Indian Territory had the problem of patching up the differences between those who had

A delegation of Southern Plains Native Americans visits in the White House conservatory during the Civil War, March 27, 1863. The white woman standing at the far right is thought to be Mary Todd Lincoln.

fought on opposing sides during the war. Once that had been done, they then had to make their peace with the victorious Union.

The tribes, after making peace with each other, were shocked when the U.S. government representatives began treating them all as enemies, even those who had fought on the side of the Union.

Eventually new treaties were signed, but, under them, the Five Civilized Tribes and others had to give up some of their lands and also agree to allow railroads to be built across their territory. The westward advance of the white settler continued.

Curriculum Context

Many curricula ask students to identify and analyze events leading up to outright conflict.

The American Revolutionary War

The American Revolutionary War was fought between 1775 and 1783. Britain was defeated in the war, and most of the former British colonies in North America gained their independence to become the United States of America.

Curriculum Context

Many curricula ask students to recognize how European groups viewed the cultures they encountered in the course of their explorations and settlements.

When the war began, both the British and the Revolutionaries, also known as Colonials or Patriots, realized that Native Americans could provide military support to their armies. Generally, the Patriots tried to persuade Native Americans to stay out of the fighting. Some did, but others sided with the British and began raiding American settlements. The raids in Pennsylvania were fierce. In July 1778 over 350 Patriot soldiers were killed in a battle known as the Wyoming Valley Massacre.

Militia

A body of private citizens called upon for military service in times of emergency.

The Patriot militia retaliated and destroyed several Native American towns in the fall, stepping up operations even more in 1779. General John Sullivan led almost 4,000 troops from the Patriot Continental Army and a strong force of Oneida warriors into Iroquois territory. Sullivan and his troops won a battle at Elmira, New York, and went on to burn many Iroquois villages and destroy crops.

Iroquois League of Nations

An alliance of native peoples of the northeastern United States, including the Mohawk, Oneida, Onondago, Cayuga, Seneca, and Tuscarora.

The Iroquois continued their attacks in New York and Pennsylvania, but by 1782, when the Revolution ended, they had suffered terribly. In the course of the war, about one-third of the Iroquois died, mostly of disease or starvation. For those who had survived came the realization that the unity of the Iroquois League of Nations had been lost forever.

Ohio and Kentucky at war

After the start of the war, the Shawnee made destructive raids on white settlements in what are now West Virginia and Kentucky. By 1778, after the murder of a Shawnee chief named Cornstalk, most of the Shawnee had decided to fight for the British. At the same time, the Patriots were preparing an expedition, led by George Rogers Clark, to capture Fort Vincennes in Indiana and

Native Americans were involved in many battles during the American Revolution. The battles labeled here were some of the more important of those conflicts.

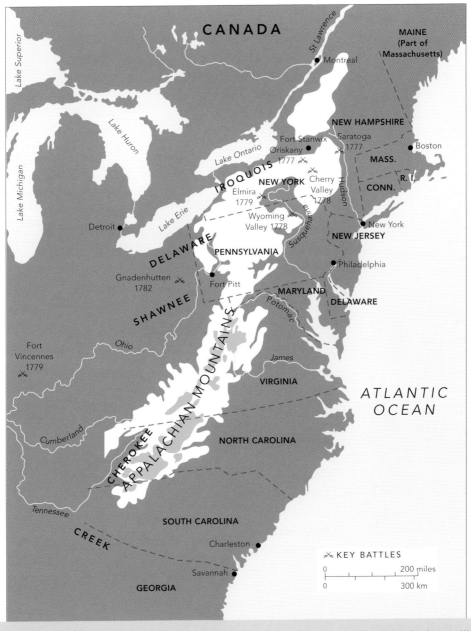

CANADA

MAINE
(Part of
Massachusetts)

Lake Superior

St Lawrence

Montreal

Lake Huron

NEW HAMPSHIRE

Fort Stanwix   Saratoga
Oriskany   1777   Boston
1777
MASS.

Lake Ontario

Lake Michigan

IROQUOIS

Cherry
Elmira   NEW YORK   Valley
1779   1778   CONN.   R. I.

Hudson

Detroit   Lake Erie

Wyoming
Valley 1778   New York

Susquehanna

NEW JERSEY

DELAWARE

PENNSYLVANIA

Philadelphia

Gnadenhutten
1782   Fort Pitt   MARYLAND

Potomac

DELAWARE

SHAWNEE

Ohio   James

Fort
Vincennes   VIRGINIA
1779
APPALACHIAN MOUNTAINS

ATLANTIC
OCEAN

Cumberland

CHEROKEE

NORTH CAROLINA

Tennessee

CREEK   SOUTH CAROLINA

Charleston   KEY BATTLES

0   200 miles
Savannah
0   300 km
GEORGIA

Famous frontiersman Daniel Boone was captured by Native Americans during fighting in 1778.

then, they hoped, Detroit. Detroit was the base of the British leader Henry Hamilton, "the Hair Buyer," who paid Native Americans to take scalps from the Patriots whom they killed.

The fighting in 1778 was indecisive, though the Shawnee did capture the noted pioneer Daniel Boone, who had led the first white settlers into Kentucky. In February 1779 Clark and his troops finally took Vincennes. Many Shawnee and Delaware villages were destroyed by other Patriot attacks later that year.

The Delaware people made a treaty with the new United States at Fort Pitt (now Pittsburgh, Pennsylvania) on September 17, 1778—the first made by the U.S. government with Native Americans. The treaty did not last long, however. In 1782 a band of peaceful Delaware was massacred by frontiersmen at Gnadenhutten, a settlement in Ohio.

Curriculum Context

Many curricula ask students to analyze the different perspectives of Native Americans and white settlers in the American Revolution, and to examine why many Native Americans remained loyal to the British.

Bering Bridge

It is thought that the first settlers of the Americas came from Asia. At the end of the Pleistocene era, which lasted from 1,600,000 to 10,000 years ago, nomadic hunters crossed from Siberia to Alaska. At this time a huge amount of water was locked in massive ice sheets, lowering sea levels as much as 280 feet (85 m) and exposing a plateau in the region of the Bering Strait.

This plateau, the Bering Bridge, linked parts of Siberia with an ice-free passage via the Yukon into interior North America. The Bering Bridge, which was 620 miles (1,000 km) at its widest, allowed people to move between the two continents. Scholars do not agree about when the first migrations took place.

Going back in time

Until recently it was believed that humans did not enter the North American continent until 5,000 years ago—and some scholars claimed people could not have arrived earlier than 2,000 years ago. This view was based mainly on the fact that no remains of early humans had been found in America. All evidence suggested the first Native American populations were of the modern human genus *Homo sapiens*.

Then, in 1926, a team of archaeologists at Folsom, New Mexico, discovered spearheads embedded in the remains of *Bison antiquus*. This Ice Age bison became extinct during the closing of the Pleistocene some 10,000 years ago. Here was proof that hunting populations had coexisted with the last of the Ice Age mammals.

Other evidence gives earlier dates. Carbon 14 dating—a method of measuring the slow loss of radioactivity from organic material—shows dates of more than 30,000 years ago. Unconfirmed evidence suggests dates as long ago as 80,000 years.

Curriculum Context

For many curricula, students are asked to draw upon data provided by archaeologists and geologists to explain the origins and migration from Asia to the Americas.

Pleistocene

A period of geologic time lasting roughly from 2 million years ago to 10,000 years ago; humans appeared during this epoch.

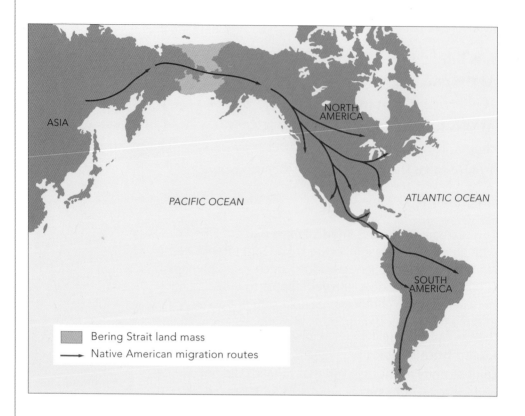

Bering Strait land mass
Native American migration routes

From Asia, small bands of hunters took advantage of the Bering Strait land bridge, which joined Siberia to Alaska, to travel into North America. Over the centuries, the new emigrants slowly moved across the continent and into South America. This map estimates those early movements.

A drawbridge in history

The Bering Bridge provides its own clues to dating the migration. Although finding evidence of early human activity in the region is almost impossible since it now lies buried beneath the waters of the Bering Strait, geographic surveys reveal that the "bridge" was open at specific periods during the Pleistocene era, which lasted for nearly 1.5 million years. The first period was 80,000–70,000 years ago; then 35,000–20,000 years ago; and the last was 12,000–10,000 years ago.

Modern humans evolved outside of the Americas some 40,000–50,000 years ago. This, taken together with other evidence, suggests a probable date for the first migrations across the Bering Bridge during the middle "open" period, about 35,000 years ago. Earlier dates seem unlikely because of the lack of verified evidence of pre-*Homo sapiens* in either North or South America.

Bureau of Indian Affairs

The Bureau of Indian Affairs (or BIA) was created in 1824. Its original purpose was, in the words of John Caltham, U.S. secretary of war in 1824, "to civilize the Indians." The BIA regulated and administered laws and treaties that affected Native Americans.

Fledgling years

At first the BIA was primarily concerned with waging and winning wars against the Native Americans in order to ease western expansion. And so it remained until 1849, when the Department of Interior took over the bureau from the War Department. After this change from military to civil control, the bureau was reorganized into several sections. Each section answered to the commissioner of Indian affairs, who headed the BIA. The commissioner, in turn, answered to the U.S. secretary of the interior and, ultimately, to the president.

The bureau grew quickly in its early years and underwent several reorganizations. Such a big enterprise needed many workers to make it function, including interpreters, lawyers, architects, and financial clerks. By 1910 some 5,000 employees worked in the BIA. By 1934—when the BIA's budget was drastically increased—that figure had risen to 12,000.

The departments

The BIA was organized in several divisions that managed a range of aspects dealing with Native Americans. A fieldwork division dealt with problems of irrigation, assisting Native Americans to find employment, and the prosecution of liquor sales on reservations. A land division dealt with allotment, sale of lands and concessions, and guarded reservation borders against settlers' attempts to trespass. This

Curriculum Context

Many curricula outline the need for students to understand the political, economic, and social changes in the United States in the mid to late 1800s.

should have protected tribes from abuse, but in practice it severely restricted other native people's access to the reservations and isolated those who lived on them.

Curriculum Context

Often curricula expect that the student can analyze political issues, such as Native American policies, within the context of the time period in which they arise.

Contacts with people outside the reservations were mostly restricted to the official visits of the bureau's commissioners such as the schools superintendent. The schools superintendent managed the education division, which was in charge of building schools for Native Americans on the reservations. The superintendent also decided where schools should be built and was responsible for hiring teachers. None of the teachers was Native American because it was thought that Native American traditions should not be preserved. The superintendent also chose all the books that Native American students used and decided on teaching methods.

Major change

After several budget increases in the early 20th century, the BIA suffered major cutbacks to its finances during the 1930s, when the economy was damaged by the Great Depression. Despite the cutbacks, the commissioner of Indian affairs at that time, John Collier, worked to change the politics of the department. He wanted to end the allotment policy and revive Native American traditions. These changes were called the Indian New Deal, in line with President Franklin D. Roosevelt's wider-ranging New Deal policies.

Although the idea was to make Native Americans more responsible for their own future, only 92 out of 258 tribes adopted the type of constitutional government proposed by the new law.

The modern bureau

In 1949 the bureau's structure was changed once again into what became the basis of the modern BIA.

In this 1870 newspaper drawing, President Ulysses S. Grant greets Chiefs Red Cloud, Spotted Tail, and Swift Bear during their visit with Ely S. Parker, the commissioner of Indian Affairs. Parker was the first Native American to hold the position.

Curriculum Context

Many curricula ask students to explain the influence of leaders of a particular time.

Increasingly, direct control over reservations was given to Native Americans themselves. This was achieved by sending federal money to the tribal governments, which were then free from the strict spending controls of the BIA. This new approach was encouraged by President John F. Kennedy in the 1960s and was called self-determination.

Self-determination
Freedom to control one's own direction or goverment.

From the 1930s more and more Native Americans were employed by the BIA. In 1960 an Oneida was appointed commissioner of Indian affairs (nearly a hundred years after the first Native American, Ely Parker, served in the post). BIA chiefs from then on had to be of Native American descent with experience of Native American life.

By 1980 the BIA had many Native Americans in more important jobs. Many aspects of tribal life that were once the responsibility of the BIA were now under Native American control. Today the BIA's 16,000 staff still has responsibility for Native American land, economic development, and education.

Cattle Trails

European settlers who began exploring the New World used, for the most part, paths and trails that Native Americans had already forged. In the East these trails were usually relatively short and linked tribal villages. In the West the trails were much longer, having been used by tribes to follow migrating buffalo herds.

Curriculum Context

Many curricula ask the student to understand the impact of political boundaries that cut across culture regions.

The trails covered an enormous area that included most of what are now the western and midwestern United States, Canada, and Mexico. The trails were very useful to the pioneers because they cut across large portions of land that were unknown to Europeans.

Ranchers seized trails

In the 19th century, as the West was being settled by ranchers and farmers, these Native American and pioneer trails became cattle trails. In many cases they were the most convenient and direct routes. They connected the vast ranches to railroad towns hundreds of miles away, where the cattle could be transported to the large and populous cities back East.

Chisholm Trail

One of the famous cattle trails of the 1800s. Jesse Chisholm, half Scottish and half Cherokee, drove a load of buffalo hides from San Antonio, Texas, to Abilene, Kansas, for trading. The weight of his wagon left deep wheel ruts in the ground that others later followed to make the same journey.

Sometimes new trails were forged. In 1866 the part-Cherokee trader Jesse Chisholm drove a wagon train of buffalo hides across the southern plains between Kansas and Texas. For the next 20 years, his trail was the favored route of cowboys driving their cattle herds from San Antonio to Abilene. The route became known as the Chisholm Trail. Other commonly used cattle trails ran both west and east from this famous path.

End of a hunting tradition

Cattle trails were in part responsible for the disappearance of the buffalo herds and other wild animals on which Native American existence depended. The huge herds of cattle passing through the Great Plains disturbed the pastures and migratory patterns of buffalo, antelope, and deer. This meant that Native Americans could no longer rely on the game that they had traditionally hunted.

Some of the groups that were the most affected included the Arapaho, Cheyenne, Sioux, Comanche, Kiowa, and Crow. The dispersal of the buffalo forced many to move to new hunting grounds. This meant they were soon encroaching on other nations' lands.

The hunt for land created friction and resentment, and animosity grew between the hunting tribes. Cattle trails then began to attract Native Americans searching for food or responding to military attacks. The U.S. government saw this as a threat to the settlers, and several military campaigns were organized by the army in order to defend the herds and herders.

Curriculum Context

Curricula often ask students to describe how various Indian Nations lived and adjusted to the natural environment.

The four main cattle trails were the Western, Chisholm, Shawnee, and Goodnight-Loving. These trails helped ranchers move their livestock to market. They also disrupted Native American life.

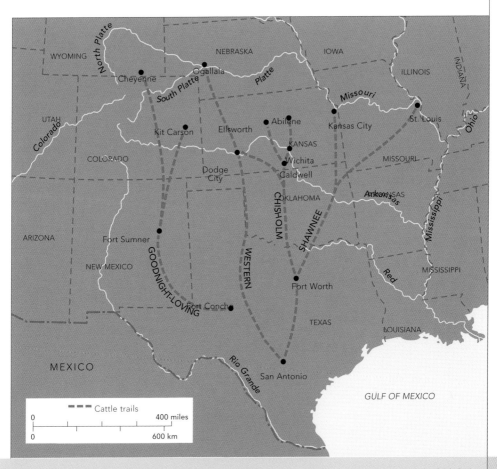

Disenfranchisement

Disenfranchisement is the removal of an individual's or group's human and legal rights. Most Native American demands for rights today relate to old, unresolved disputes arising from treaties and from rights that might have been granted under those treaties but that Native Americans feel they have now lost.

Native American attempts to reclaim their rights are often frustrated by the vague terms of the original treaties. At the time these agreements were made, many Native Americans could not read. Interpreters were used, but they were often biased toward European or U.S. interests. As a result, Native Americans often signed treaties that did not give them what they expected.

Conversion to Christianity

Native American disenfranchisement took many forms. One example was the enforced replacement of native religious beliefs by European ones. The Spanish missions in California and the Southwest, for instance, recognized natives as human beings. A papal decree declared Native Americans had souls to be saved. But the souls had to be converted to Christianity in order to be saved. This resulted in brutal religious persecution.

European contact

French contact with Native Americans was based on trade. The cooperation of native people was vital to French trading efforts. Alliances were cemented by planned marriages between leading traders and the families of local chiefs. This meant that people who came into important tribal positions through marriage would promote French interests, not those of their fellow Native Americans.

British policy was concerned with settlement, and treaty agreements were based on this. In these agreements

Native Americans gave up territory in return for guarantees of limited possession and use of land and water resources, hunting and fishing rights, and the right to self-government.

Protecting native rights

These treaties are regarded as still binding by most Native Americans today. The U.S. and Canadian governments are obliged by law to protect tribal possessions from violation by private citizens, the state, and local authorities. In practice, this has not been the case. The Indian Removal Act of 1830, for example, resulted in entire tribes being forced from their homelands and settled in the Indian Territory, supposedly to "protect and safeguard" their interests.

The 1887 Dawes General Allotment Act then broke up these tribally owned reservations into individual plots. These plots were large enough for small-scale farming but not for traditional hunting economies. Native families, reluctant to accept foreign methods of subsistence or to live in areas unsuitable for farming, sold or leased their lands.

Curriculum Context

A study and comparison of the relationships between Native Americans and French, British, Spanish, and Dutch settlers is included in many curricula.

This map shows the Native American land surrendered first to the Europeans and later to the Americans up to the end of the 19th century.

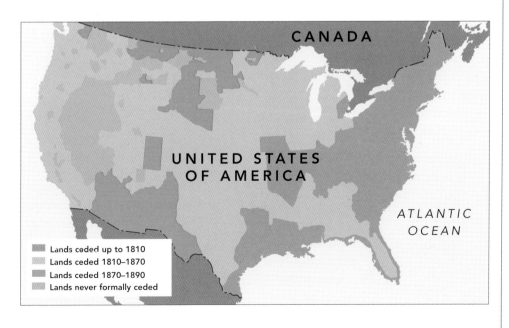

CANADA

UNITED STATES
OF AMERICA

ATLANTIC
OCEAN

▨ Lands ceded up to 1810
▨ Lands ceded 1810–1870
▨ Lands ceded 1870–1890
▨ Lands never formally ceded

Education

Before the Europeans arrived in North America, there were no formal schools for Native American children. Since there were no written languages, there were no books, and children learned by being shown and told how to do things.

Education was largely a matter of passing on practical skills, such as hunting, basket making, or growing crops. Children also learned through repeating the stories, songs, poems, and dances that made up a people's store of history, folklore, beliefs, and culture.

There were no full-time teachers. Children learned mainly from their parents. In tribes organized by a clan system, other relatives, such as the mother's brother, might take special responsibility for a child's teaching. Children would also learn a great deal from their grandparents. They learned through instruction and through practicing skills in play.

In some tribes children were supervised and taught all the time. Generally, though, children learned from whomever could teach them. The best hunters, warriors, and craftspeople passed on their special skills, while the tribal shaman and the village elders were sometimes responsible for the spiritual education of young people. Those destined to become a chief, shaman, or other important person received special attention.

Becoming an adult

The nearest thing to a test in traditional Native American education occurs in those tribes in which children must go through a series of rituals and ceremonies in order to become adults. Both boys and girls usually have to go through this testing. The ceremonies involve some spiritual teaching and a period of close contact between young people and their teacher. During this period the educator instructs the young people in the proper ways to behave in order to be good members of their society. Grandmothers and older women who are thought of as wise usually instruct young girls, while grandfathers and old men teach the boys.

The education of young people in many Plains societies was typical of this traditional approach. Young men were, and still are, taken to secluded places in order to search for a spiritual vision—a practice known as Vision Quest. This difficult and important time in a young man's life involves a period of fasting and long hours of concentration, rather like meditation. During this time he will, it is believed, learn principles that will guide him throughout his life.

The initiation ceremony for Apache girls requires them to go through a series of long and difficult steps similar to those of the Plains natives' Vision Quest. Assisted by older, knowledgable women, they have to dance and run for long periods. Throughout the four-day ceremony, the girls are taught traditional values and are blessed, in the hope they will grow up to be honorable women.

A mission to instruct

Christian missions set up by the Spanish colonists brought European-style education to North America. The main task of the missionaries was to convert the native peoples to European values and the Christian religion. In mission schools, the natives were taught to read so that they could study the Bible. Missions were eventually set up throughout North America.

Assimilation

The next drive sought to give native children a more formal European education outside the missions. It began at the end of the 18th century and continued

Curriculum Context

Many curricula ask students to make a comparative study of gender roles in European and Native American societies.

Vision Quest

A rite of passage in many Native American groups, in which young individuals go alone to an isolated place to seek protection from the spirits.

Into the 19th century. During this time the U.S. government forced Native Americans to send their children to government schools, where all lessons were taught in English. Native American children were removed from their homes, often by force, and sent far away from their parents for years to stop them from having any contact with their traditional culture.

Such schools were set up to put into practice the theories of assimilationists. These people believed that the only way to solve the "Indian problem" was to destroy the various native cultures and absorb the people into mainstream American culture.

The assimilationist philosophy led to schools in which Native American children were forbidden to speak their own language or wear tribal clothing. If they did either, they were punished—perhaps severely beaten—for disobedience. The assimilation policy peaked with the Carlisle Indian School in Pennsylvania. Hundreds of native children attended this institution, which was founded by Richard H. Pratt in 1879.

In the 19th century, the education division of the Bureau of Indian Affairs (BIA) took responsibility for building schools on reservations. By 1900 half of all Native American children attended BIA schools. The BIA schools also followed an assimilationist line. All native children were given a European Christian education, and they were still forced to learn the English language. The BIA would often recruit religious groups to build schools and teach on reservations.

Resistance and reform

The way that their heritage and cultural traditions were deliberately discouraged led many Native American groups to resist the system that had been imposed on them by the government. In 1887, for example, the Keam's Canyon Hopi government school was deserted

because parents refused to send their children there. The first school to be run by Native Americans for Native Americans was the American Indian Institute, founded in Kansas in 1915 by Henry Roe Cloud, a Winnebago. In 1935 Navajo, Sioux, and Pueblo schools began offering lessons in native languages as well as English.

In the last 50 years, Native Americans have largely taken control of their children's education, and the BIA has changed policy after being criticized for showing insufficient respect for native traditions. New plans have been made to suit native students from different tribes. Each area now has its own tribal schools, and the courses encourage the teaching and learning of native languages, oral history, traditions, and social values. In this way it is hoped that people will start to regain a sense of their cultural identity.

In this photo, taken around 1905, a group of Native Americans gathers for the initiation of one of their young men.

Oral history

The passing of one's culture through story-telling and memory.

Epidemics

Disease introduced by European settlers had a devastating effect on Native Americans. Epidemics of diseases, such as smallpox, claimed the lives of millions, far more than those killed in warfare.

A lack of resistance

The reason for the epidemics is simple: Native Americans had no resistance to diseases from Europe because they had never been exposed to them before. From the early 16th to the late 19th centuries, all tribes suffered severely, some more than others. For example, 92 percent of the Mandan of the Upper Missouri River were wiped out in 1837 due to smallpox.

The groups that suffered most were those living along the Atlantic Coast and the edge of the Gulf of Mexico. These people were the first to come in contact with the Europeans. From there European diseases spread west. Airborne diseases, such as smallpox, spread faster than other contact diseases like cholera.

However, in all cases, diseases were spread by people, and wherever people traveled, there was a danger of infection. Native American camps situated along the trade routes used by white traders and settlers were most at risk. As the trade routes moved deeper into the continent of North America, so too did disease.

Smallpox was the most devastating disease, with some tribes experiencing epidemics several times within a few years. Other European diseases that killed many Native Americans included measles, scarlet fever, typhoid, influenza, and tuberculosis. By the 19th century, as methods of transportation improved, rapid movement of people caused a new wave of epidemics. This time

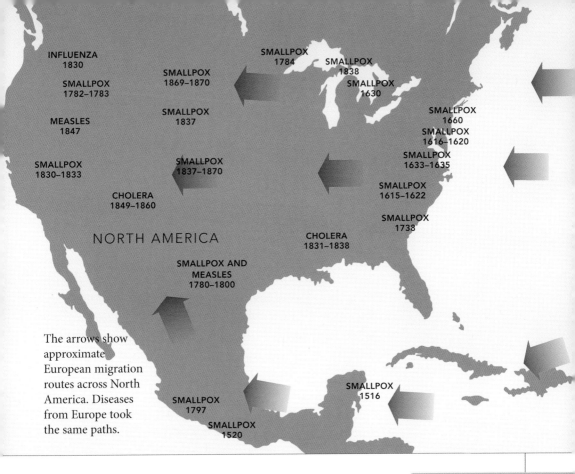

INFLUENZA
1830

SMALLPOX
1782–1783

SMALLPOX
1869–1870

SMALLPOX
1784

SMALLPOX
1838

SMALLPOX
1630

MEASLES
1847

SMALLPOX
1837

SMALLPOX
1660

SMALLPOX
1616–1620

SMALLPOX
1830–1833

SMALLPOX
1837–1870

SMALLPOX
1633–1635

CHOLERA
1849–1860

SMALLPOX
1615–1622

NORTH AMERICA

CHOLERA
1831–1838

SMALLPOX
1738

SMALLPOX AND
MEASLES
1780–1800

The arrows show approximate European migration routes across North America. Diseases from Europe took the same paths.

SMALLPOX
1797

SMALLPOX
1520

SMALLPOX
1516

peoples of the Plains and Plateau regions were badly affected and their populations decimated. Since epidemics claimed so many lives, there were few individuals left to take up hereditary positions of leadership. As a result, many tribal traditions and rules changed to accommodate the needs of those who were left.

Curriculum Context

Many curricula emphasize the importance of understanding the relationship of cause and effect.

War and disease

During Pontiac's War (1763–1764), the British fought an alliance of tribes. British Captain Simeon Ecuyer gave blankets to the warriors he was fighting. The blankets were infected with smallpox, which caused an epidemic among the local tribes. Although Ecuyer gained time for his British reinforcements to arrive, his methods have since been judged negatively.

Extinction

The word *extinction* means "the complete disappearance of something." We use it to refer to Native American tribes whose unique way of life, culture, and language no longer exist. Many tribes lived in North America when Europeans first began to settle the continent. Of those, as many as half have become extinct.

Curriculum Context

For some curricula, students are asked to describe the internecine Indian conflicts, including the competing claims for control of lands and the results of those conflicts.

There are many complex reasons for extinction. Sometimes they had little to do with Europeans. Some small groups in competition with larger, more aggressive neighbors found themselves unable to secure everything they needed for survival. To protect themselves they often joined together in confederacies that, after some time, became new tribes with customs, and sometimes languages, different from those of the original groups.

Other small groups became allies of their neighbors, gradually adopting the dress, customs, and language of the larger tribe. In this way their own unique cultures disappeared even though the people themselves had not died out.

The end of whole tribes

Sometimes, however, whole tribes did become extinct. This usually happened to small groups living in areas where life was difficult. A series of harsh winters, crop failures, or lack of success in hunting could mean whole communities starved to death, and with them their language and way of life disappeared forever.

When Europeans arrived, the pattern of extinction changed dramatically. Sometimes this was because the Europeans wanted Native American lands. Armed only with bows and arrows, spears, and clubs, many tribes were unable to fight back effectively against the Europeans' muskets and cannons. Their people were massacred, and whole tribes became extinct.

At times the Europeans bribed other Native American groups to fight for them. For example, the Beothuk of Newfoundland resisted the English and the French. So the Europeans gave guns to the Beothuk's traditional enemies, the Micmac, and paid them a bounty for every Beothuk scalp they took. After a long and one-sided war, the Beothuk were defeated. Only a few refugees survived and fled to other tribes for protection, adopting their customs and languages.

Curriculum Context

Many curricula challenge students to analyze the impact of European presence and influence.

Epidemics from Europe

Europeans also brought diseases with them to which Native Americans had no immunity. Smallpox was the most deadly of these, and epidemics killed up to 90 percent of some tribal populations. With their numbers so dramatically reduced, the tribes were unable to defend themselves and the loss of their chiefs and ritual leaders meant many customs died out. With the remnants of the tribes scattered, their languages and cultures vanished.

Shanawdithit was the last known survivor of the Beothuk people. She was a servant in the household of William Eppes Cormack, who recorded stories that she told him of the Beothuk. He also collected her drawings illustrating the Beothuk way of life. Shanawdithit died of tuberculosis in 1829.

Fishing Rights

In the 19th century, most Native Americans were moved onto reservations, completely disrupting their way of life. Native Americans had often depended on hunting and fishing for survival, and many of the original treaties that forced them onto reservations safeguarded hunting and fishing. However, the ability to fish freely was soon limited by regulations.

The situation today is very different, but problems remain. Fishing rights involve federal, state, and tribal administrations. Tribal governments have established fishing cooperatives to keep their traditional economy alive and benefit from small-scale exports. The issue has also been of great importance in Native American politics and continues to spark dissent and protest when peoples' interests are ignored or abused.

Problems with fishing rights in recent years have given rise to "fish-ins" as a form of protest against fishing restrictions. In 1959 Alaskan natives benefited from the introduction of a system that considered residency and size of income in determining the right to fish. Other examples include rights to salmon fishing along spawning rivers on the Northwest Coast, which have been eroded by the offshore fishing activities of commercial fishermen. This led to a series of fish-ins along rivers in Washington state in 1964 organized by the National Indian Youth Council.

Commercial fishermen
Those who fish as a source of income.

Rights vs. equality

Because fishing occupies an important place in their culture, Native Americans believe they should have special status in the allocation of fishing rights. The U.S. government, on the other hand, does not want to grant this on the basis that it would contradict the principle of equality. Who can and who cannot fish is a delicate issue that continues to cause controversy.

Folsom and Clovis

Folsom, a village in northeastern New Mexico, is an important archaeological site a few miles north of Capulin Volcano and east of Dead Horse Gulch. Folsom became famous when in 1908 George McJunkin, an archaeologist exploring a site there, discovered the bones of an extinct long-horned bison, *Bison antiquus*.

Excavations of the site from 1926 to 1928 uncovered spear tips embedded between the ribs of other *Bison antiquus* bones. The flint tips were leaf-shaped, with fluted sides for attaching to a spear shaft.

At the time, archaeologists and historians believed that humans had inhabited North America for about 4,000 years. The tips, found to be over 10,000 years old, provided the first serious evidence that humans were hunting animals on the continent from the last Ice Age, which ended 10,000 years ago.

The large number of bones found at the site indicated that Folsom was a "kill site" used by Paleo-Indians. These early Indians, who were hunter–gatherers, came to the region because of the abundance of large game that provided food, shelter, and clothing. Kill sites were usually near creeks or water holes. A group of hunters would set up camp on high ground to watch for animals coming to drink at the water below. The hunters would then drive the animals into boggy ground and spear them as they struggled in the mud.

Blackwater Draw, Clovis

At Blackwater Draw, near Clovis in southeastern New Mexico, other flint tips were discovered in 1932. They were smaller, with deeper flutes and cruder than those at Folsom. Archaeologists believe they are about 2,000 years older than the Folsom tips.

Curriculum Context

Curricula often highlight the work of archaeologists who gain understanding of a culture by analyzing even the smallest of clues.

Paleo-Indians

Nomadic hunting people who first inhabited North America; archaeological evidence suggests these people came into existence in the late Pleistocene.

French and Indian War

The French and Indian War, which lasted from 1754 until 1763, was a conflict between France and Britain, with Native Americans as allies on both sides. The Europeans fought for control of North America. The Native Americans of the North and Southeast fought each other in part to settle old scores but mostly because of manipulation by France and Britain.

Curriculum Context

Many curricula challenge students to analyze the impact of European presence and influence.

French and Indian War

A war (1754–1763) fought between Britain and France and their respective native allies for colonial supremacy in North America. British victory was confirmed in the Treaty of Paris in 1763.

Fierce conflict

It was a brutal conflict, but most of the casualties were caused in small raids on frontier farms and villages. Houses, crops, and farm animals were burned or killed, and peaceable civilians—white settlers and Native Americans—were murdered or driven off their lands by groups of both white and native attackers.

In previous wars between Britain and France, the fighting in North America took place within New England and in upstate New York. In the French and Indian War, the fighting involved those areas and the Ohio Valley, Pennsylvania, Maryland, and Virginia.

In 1752 the Virginia authorities negotiated a treaty with Iroquois leaders, granting them land on which to build a fort. The French struck back in 1753 by building a chain of forts of their own to regain control of the local trade and keep out the British. In 1754 a young officer from Virginia named George Washington was sent to expel the French from Fort Duquesne (modern Pittsburgh), but his small army was defeated. This was the start of the war; all-out fighting began in 1755.

For the first few years of the war, the British suffered heavy defeats. Despite having a greater population in North America than the French, the British were badly organized and poorly commanded. However, at the end of 1756, William Pitt took over at the head of the British government in London and set about turning the war around. Pitt's most important decision was to arrange a bargain with Anglo-American colonists. He promised to provide sufficient funds to wage the war in North America if the colonists would raise the soldiers.

Turning of the tide

At this same time, some of the French and Native American alliances began to unravel. In 1758 the British negotiated a treaty with the Iroquois. The British returned land they had previously taken and promised to stay out of it in the future. Although the promise was short-lived, it was enough for the Iroquois, the Delaware, and other tribes to stop helping the French.

Legacy of a British victory

Without their allies, the French were in trouble. After a series of defeats, the French governor in Canada surrendered completely in 1760. The Treaty of Paris ended the war in 1763 and confirmed that Britain would keep control of Canada and the other British colonies. Native Americans from then on would not get help from the French when they wanted to stop the British from taking their lands. And despite the help they had been given by Native Americans in the war, the British went back to doing just that.

Curriculum Context

Curricula may ask students to analyze the nature of Native American and European alliances.

An engraving depicting a battle of the French and Indian War shows the defeat of General Edward Braddock in Virginia in 1755.

Ghost Dance

The Ghost Dance was a Native American cult that originated among the Paiute in the late 19th century. These people lived in two tribes in the Great Basin, the area between the Rocky Mountains and the Sierra Nevada range, most of which is in the state of Nevada.

Most Native Americans believed that some men and women had the special ability to contact the spirit world and make use of the power it held. People with this talent were described by white settlers in the 18th and 19th centuries as medicine men and women, and are known today as shamans.

On New Year's Day, 1889, Nevada was the site of a solar eclipse that plunged the whole area into darkness. At the same time, a Paiute shaman named Wovoka was suffering from a high fever. He later said that the fever had broken at the beginning of the eclipse. At that exact moment, he claimed, he entered the spirit world, where he learned of a new world to come for all Native Americans. This new world would be brought about by fasting and performing a ritual called the Ghost Dance.

An apocalyptic vision

Wovoka's message and the Ghost Dance cult borrowed heavily from Christian beliefs, including the ending of the existing world and its replacement by a new one. Wovoka foretold that if Native Americans fasted and performed the Ghost Dance, they would bring to an end the world of the white people and restore the traditional world of Native America.

The Ghost Dance cult effectively opened the world of the shaman to all Native Americans who chose to follow Wovoka's teachings. Before, only shamans performed ritual dances and chanted incantations to exert their

Curriculum Context

The influence and achievements of significant leaders of various Native American groups is addressed by many curricula.

Apocalyptic
A prediction of immense disaster.

An illustration of Sioux people engaged in a Ghost Dance captures some of the fervor of the ceremony.

power. However, every Native American could participate in the Ghost Dance, and anyone who took part would be able to enter the spirit world and contact the souls of the dead.

The Ghost Dance was a remarkable ceremony. The dancing sometimes went on for several days, with only brief pauses to rest. Some would pass out, and when revived, they would speak of their brief stays in the spirit world and of what they saw there.

Curriculum Context

Many curricula encourage students to describe the connections between the religious beliefs of a people and the rituals that they build.

Rapid rise and fall

The Ghost Dance cult spread rapidly among western tribes in 1890. The U.S. government feared that this would lead to a pantribal uprising, despite Wovoka's pacifist message. That same year, along a creek in South Dakota called Wounded Knee, U.S. troops massacred 350 Sioux who were wearing Ghost Dance shirts supposed to protect them from the soldier's bullets. The massacre marked the end of the Ghost Dance, and of the independence of Native Americans.

Hudson's Bay Company

Set up in 1668, the Hudson's Bay Company greatly expanded the trade in furs between Native Americans and Europeans throughout northern North America. It also gave Britain a powerful base in Canada. Previously, French and British traders had individually exchanged European goods for furs with Native Americans.

Curriculum Context

Many curricula challenge students to analyze the motivation and ambition of the European nations.

Hudson Bay

The body of water located in northeastern Canada named after the explorer Henry Hudson. The bay connects to the Atlantic Ocean on the east via the Hudson strait and the Arctic Ocean to the north. Discovery of this waterway led to the formation of the British owned Hudson's Bay Company, which greatly aided the fur trade with the Cree people.

Both the British and French governments were eager to control the fur trade as a way of gaining huge new territories and making money. To try to corner the market, the French set up exchange posts, but their harsh pricing and creation of false competition angered the individual traders.

Founding the company

Two Frenchmen, Pierre Radisson and Médard de Groseilliers, who had established trading links with the Cree and Huron, were fined by France for unlicensed trading. The two men, angry at their own government, turned to Britain for help. With the financial backing of Prince Rupert—cousin of King Charles II—and a group of adventurers and noblemen, they set up the Hudson's Bay Company and sailed to James Bay (the southern offshoot of Hudson Bay). Two years later, in 1670, they returned to Britain with a ship full of furs, which they sold for a large profit.

As a result, Charles II granted the company a royal charter, giving it sole rights to settle and trade along the coast of Hudson Bay and James Bay and to exploit the surrounding area. Within 10 years the Hudson's Bay Company had forts on the mouths of the Rupert, Moose, and Albany rivers in James Bay and was trading profitably with Native Americans. The formation of the Hudson's Bay Company inevitably increased the tension between the French and the British. A year after the company was established, a French priest called Father Marquette founded a mission, St. Ignace, on the Straits of Mackinac between Lake Michigan and Lake Huron. The French then claimed the entire Northeast.

In 1697 French forces captured most of the company's bases, leaving it only the fort at Albany. The company was nearly ruined, but its bases were returned under the Treaty of Utrecht in 1713.

Tribal conflict

As the conflict between the French and the British escalated, both sides formed alliances with Native Americans. As a result, the Cree and Assiniboine started driving the Sioux from the north. The Ojibway, fearing they would lose their interests in the fur trade, joined in the effort to move the Sioux westward, away from their own territory. In the mid-1700s the Sioux turned from being farmers to horse breeders in order to defend themselves better. They acquired horses from the Arikara, settled on the northern Plains, and became one of the dominant tribes in the region.

In 1763, following their victory over the French in the French and Indian War, Britain took control of Canada. At this time the Hudson's Bay Company started building bases inland to the west because of increasing competition from small trading companies. In 1783 several small rivals formed the Northwest Company, which in 1805 established the first trading post west of the Rockies.

Curriculum Context

Curricula may ask students to identify factors that contribute to cooperation and conflict between individuals or peoples.

Companies with long lives

Competition between the Hudson Bay and Northwest companies was so fierce that the British made them merge under the Hudson's Bay Company's name. The company still operates in Canada and is active in retailing, real estate, and resource development.

Indian Claims Commission

Because they have dealt with the U.S. legal system for more than a century, Native Americans have had many opportunities to test their claims for land in courts and tribunals. They have negotiated with several different legal institutions, one of which has been the Indian Claims Commission.

The commission was set up in a final attempt to solve the several hundred cases that its predecessor, the Court of Claims, had been unable to resolve since the late 18th century. In the 20th century, Native Americans came to depend on this new, special commission to negotiate and manage the judicial claims and territorial disputes raised by the peoples living on reservations.

New citizens

In 1924 Native Americans officially became citizens, with the right to vote. Two decades later the end of World War II brought with it many changes in American society. After their active participation in the war as U.S. soldiers, many Native Americans expected some form of recognition for their commitment to the United States. Many in government also felt it was the right time to try to make amends for the unjust way Native Americans had been treated in the past, and in recognition of this the Indian Claims Commission was created in 1946.

The creation of the commission was due in part to the support of the National Congress of American Indians (NCAI). This Native American group had formed with the intention of defending tribal rights in the courts. The commission was effectively a court, and native nations had to prove their identity as a tribe before it would consider their case. This set the standard for the modern legal battles of Native Americans over land disputes and questions of tribal recognition.

Processing of claims

In 1947, one year after its official opening, the commission became effective and started processing more than 300 outstanding cases. An initial 10-year period of life for the commission was approved to resolve all the cases. However, it soon became clear that 10 years would not be enough time to complete the work required. Twice between 1956 and 1961 a renewal of the commission was approved.

By the 1960s the number of cases had more than doubled, and of those only 80 had been closed. Further renewals were approved in 1967 and 1972 to cope with the demand. And still many cases were unresolved by 1977. In 1978 it was decided that the Indian Claims Commission should pass its work on to the Court of Claims. Native American legal wrangles became very complicated and seldom successful for Native Americans. Few tribes received compensation in the way of land. Among the more successful nations was the Yakima of Washington State, who regained 21,000 acres (8,505 ha) of its land.

Native American chiefs Frank Seelatse and Chief Jimmy Noah Saluskin of the Yakima tribe stand in front of the U.S. Capitol in Washington, D.C.

Indian Territory

In 1834 land west of the boundary marked by the Mississippi River was designated by the U.S. government as Indian Territory, and Native American groups from many parts of the continent were forced in different ways to move there. The intention was for this territory to remain Native American land for ever and to end the suffering of the Native Americans.

Curriculum Context

Many curricula expect students to recognize key historical periods and patterns of change within and across cultures during those periods.

However, the increasing need for land to house the growing number of white settlers influenced government policies, and the boundaries of the allotted land moved several times during the century. The land got progressively smaller and smaller, until in 1907 it became what is now Oklahoma.

A clash of cultures

The history of this territory is linked closely to many Native American nations that mainly inhabited the eastern and southern regions of North America.

On the one hand, the territory had to host the remaining descendants of the powerful southern nations such as the Caddo, Tonkawa, Lipan Apache, and Tawakoni. Smaller groups, such as the Waco and Tawehash, had also lived there but had been progressively integrated into bigger tribes.

Integrate

To combine people from different ethnic groups or backgrounds into one common society.

On the other hand, the territory also became the homelands for the peoples of the eastern Cherokee, Delaware, Shawnee, Sauk and Fox, Kickapoo, Miami, Potawatomi, Creek, Choctaw, Chickasaw, Seminole, and Quapaw. These resettled groups had been forced out of their original lands and, inevitably, land disputes arose because other tribes had settled in the territory before them. These disputes had to be controlled with the aid of the government.

Only the resettled groups had an organized geographical location. Practically all the remaining land was unorganized territory; within it, nomadic peoples lived without fixed territory boundaries.

Each of these various groups had histories and cultures that differed greatly from one another. The U.S. government, however, gave them lands positioned without regard for tribal differences, and smaller groups were given less land. The resettled peoples found it difficult to adjust to their new surroundings because they had previously lived in very different environments. Many of them felt these changes were forced on them by the government.

Curriculum Context

Many curricula ask the student to examine and understand the impact of political boundaries that cut across culture regions.

Redesigning a nation

In 1829, when Andrew Jackson became president, the idea of resettling the tribes beyond the Mississippi gathered strength among the whites. It was made law the next year with the act of Congress named the Indian Removal Act. The act was designed to

All of the groups listed on this map were eventually forced into Indian Territory.

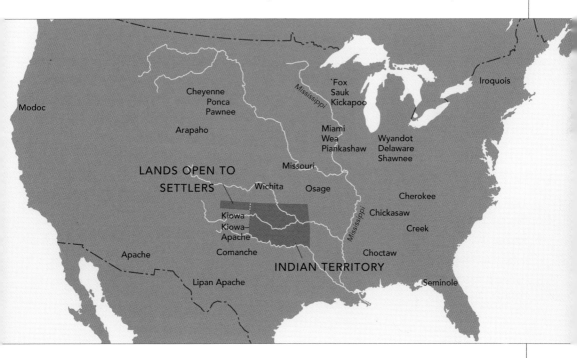

encourage new settlers. It expanded the area of potential lands to exploit and refused the Native American nations a voice in the use of the land. When the California Gold Rush started in 1848, gold miners started passing through the Indian Territory. This was only the beginning of a new era of land reductions.

Increasing tension

In 1854 the northern part of the original Indian Territory was divided into what are now Nebraska and Kansas. Both states were opened to new settlers, who could stay for five years and then own the 160 acres (64.75 ha) allotted to each homestead. To provide enough land for this scheme, the Kansas peoples were relocated, leaving less space for those already living in the Indian Territory. More Native American lands were reduced in area immediately after the Civil War (1861–65) and then until the close of the 19th century. Native people had no right of appeal against the government's decisions.

Yet more problems arose in 1845, when Texas was annexed by the United States, and more whites turned their attention to the development of the West. Some of these home seekers were known in later years as "Boomers." They were strongly supported by many commercial interests, such as developers and bankers. Their influence on Congress led to the passing in 1887 of the Dawes General Allotment Act.

The Five Civilized Tribes—Cherokee, Choctaw, Chickasaw, Creek, and Seminole—had been settled in the Indian Territory since the 1830s with treaties that promised these new lands would belong to them forever. Despite these promises the Allotment Act eventually removed the rights that the tribes had been given.

Interpreters

In 1962 an estimated 200 individual Native American languages were in active use. In Pre-Contact (before European arrival) times there were more. To complicate matters, the white settlers in the United States spoke many different languages. The largest settler language groups spoke English, French, Spanish, and German, but many other languages were spoken, too.

Interpreters were, therefore, important figures at meetings between Native American leaders and the white settlers. Sometimes a single interpreter translated directly from a Native American language into English and back again. At other times—for example, when English and Spanish speakers were present—two interpreters would be needed. Inevitably this complicated process led to changes in meaning, even when interpreters meant well. Interpreters also accidentally and even deliberately changed what was said, and inaccurate translating was often a problem in dealings between Native Americans and the U.S. Army, for example.

The situation was complicated by the fact that Native Americans did not always want to learn the settlers' languages. For example, Chief Seattle of the Squamish people refused to learn English, although he made a number of now-famous speeches to the white settlers with whom he traded.

Different backgrounds

Interpreters came from many different backgrounds. Ely Carter was a Seneca tribesman who represented his tribe in land negotiations and then became Ulysses S. Grant's trusted aide.

George Wratten, who interpreted between Geronimo and U.S. Army officers, had learned Apache while working at a reservation trading post in Apache territory.

Land Rights

The phrase "land rights" makes sense only in Western terminology. Before European contact, Native Americans had no sense of buying or owning land. It has, therefore, only been in dealings with white settlers that Native Americans have needed to think and act in such terms.

Curriculum Context

Students will be asked to examine how behaviors and beliefs of different cultures can pose barriers to crosscultural understanding.

For settled people like the Pueblo or the eastern agricultural groups, a sense of belonging to their territory was a strong part of their tribal identity. For others it was understood that territorial borders were subject to change, and people had to adjust to the circumstances that, from time to time, required moving or migrating. Land was and still is a focus in Native American religion, politics, and community, yet Native Americans view it in a different way from the whites.

In the 17th century, the English were among the first to argue that native people of North and South America had no rights to the land. In 1632 the English crown stated officially that native people could make no claims whatsoever on lands captured by "Christian princes," meaning the rulers of the European nations. The so-called purchase of Virginia from the native peoples was a trick to confuse and rob them of their land.

A sense of place

The sense of place created by the strong link with one's territory is revealed through the special connection between Native Americans and the landscape. This is important to further understand the negotiations that went on between individual tribes and the settlers. Native American landscapes speak to their inhabitants. They hold the history of the people, and they are living proof of the connection between humans and the physical world in which they live.

Each place has its own meaning. Mountains, rivers, and valleys are connected to stories that tell the history of a people. One nation may think of an area as particularly sacred because it has a special meaning for the tribe's history. It can be the place where the ancestors emerged or a particular supernatural being is said to have performed certain important actions in the nation's past. This is what gives Native Americans a strong sense of place.

Understanding this special feeling for the land also means understanding why many peoples now refuse compensation for their territory. When the Sioux were offered $10 million rather than take back the sacred Black Hills, they refused. They revere their sacred places more than money.

Other sacred places are a source of dispute and have been negotiated over as a matter of land rights. In 1990, for example, the Mohawk of New York State protested against the construction of a golf course on their sacred burial grounds, and more cases of disputes over land rights continue between the Apache and Shoshoni and the government.

Misunderstandings

Native American land rights have now emerged as a legal issue that challenges the predominant U.S. culture. It seems difficult to find a fair way to resolve the confrontations over land issues, and misunderstandings about native cultures have led to problem cases in court. This is because the original treaties were negotiated by Native American spokespeople who were not representative of their whole nation. The 1835 New Echota treaty signed by the Cherokee is one example. This Native American nation was not united over the issue of relocation, leaving a legacy of disagreement in the tribe itself.

Supernatural
Of or relating to what is beyond the natural world.

Curriculum Context
Appreciating the connections between the physical terrain and the beliefs and legends of the people living in a region will deepen understandings of Native American motivations.

New Echota treaty
A land treaty signed in 1835 by U.S. government officials and a small majority of Cherokee representatives. A large majority of Cherokees refused to acknowledge the treaty, but were forced from their lands anyway.

Curriculum Context

Concepts such as values, institutions, cohesion, diversity, accommodation, adaptation, assimilation, and dissonance—all of which are part of any study of the Native American experience—are integral to many curricula.

Cessions

The surrendering of territory.

Reclaiming land

Because Native Americans were forced to accept laws that were not theirs, the continued occupation of a piece of land by a given tribe is sometimes difficult to prove in the eyes of present-day law. Proving legal status as a tribe is important but can be difficult.

For example, the Wampanoag of Cape Cod lost their claim over 16,000 acres (6,475 ha) because they had never been listed in the official government records of where tribes lived.

Of the other eastern nations, only the Narragansett of Rhode Island won a claim in 1978 that granted them 1,800 acres (730 ha). The North Paiute and Western Shoshoni regained 2,700 acres (1,090 ha) in Nevada. However, the U.S. government has decided that the 2 billion acres (81 million ha) that were taken from Native Americans through treaties, cessions, or military intervention cannot be returned. Nevertheless, several cases are still under consideration, despite the government's 1982 Indian Claims Limitation Act.

A view of the Mittens of Monument Valley, Utah, which lie within the Navajo Nation Reservation.

Legislation

Those U.S. citizens who describe themselves as belonging to any group on the grounds of ethnic (racial) classification must satisfy certain legal requirements. In other words, people cannot simply claim to be Native American—they must prove the fact.

To prove one's heritage, a person must satisfy the requirement of "blood quantum," meaning the amount of Native American blood a person has. If this is proved, the individual will be considered by the U.S. census as a Native American.

Even then the tribal government of each reservation regulates which Native Americans are allowed membership. They can also determine who can stay on tribal property. Anyone who is not a member or who is unwelcome can be removed according to special laws. Urban Native Americans also need to register with the census, but in order to claim tribal affiliation, they depend on one or both parents' tribe of origin.

Tribes as nations

Tribes are specific and distinct political entities that in general have executive, legislative, and judicial powers. Native American sovereignty is, however, subject ultimately to federal law.

> **Sovereignty**
> Complete independence to self-govern without external influence or control.

The concept of sovereignty describes the right of states and nations to legislate on their own territory. However, this applies only partially to Native American nations, and the federal government puts limits on the regulations that each tribe can formulate. The sovereignty of the native nations is, therefore, only partial. In some ways this system resembles the restrictions that the U.S. government puts on the legislation allowed to each state of the Union.

U.S. citizens

It was only in 1924 that all Native Americans were given full U.S. citizenship, like any other American. In principle, therefore, Native Americans now have all the rights and duties of every other citizen. In regard to many issues, however, such as the selling of tribal lands, they are bound by the decisions of the Bureau of Indian Affairs (BIA).

Buying and selling property outside the reservation is not restricted by a person's ethnicity. There are thus several levels to which a Native American citizen has to respond: to federal, state, and local jurisdiction (of city or town), Bureau of Indian Affairs (BIA), and finally tribal government, each with responsibilities that may sometimes overlap.

Passport to travel

Native Americans can travel freely in and out of the reservations and travel outside the United States on American passports. However, some native nations, thanks to the sovereignty principle, do not accept these conditions and issue their own passports, such as the Hodenausee and the Iroquois League. In the past some of its tribal members have traveled with an Iroquois passport, although this is not an extensive practice.

At a local level tribes have more power to govern themselves than at the federal level. They have the right to form their own tribal legislature, regularly elected through democratic polls.

Some nations have councils; others have assemblies of adult members of the tribe as well as councils, with representatives headed by a president. As governments, tribal legislatures can make laws that can be written in the form of a constitution, or they can be oral systems.

Tribal governments regulate tribal police and have the right to solve cases that are not under federal jurisdiction. The Major Crimes Act of 1885 still defines the responsibility for major cases. Tribal legislation regulates hunting and fishing permits on tribal territory, as well as land use, and protects the reservation environment.

Responsibility for education is shared by the BIA and federal government, but some native nations have tribally operated colleges that teach traditional subjects, such as Native American history, languages, and philosophy. However, only tribes with their own sources of income can afford such educational programs because they are expensive to maintain.

Federal programs

For many other matters tribal governments depend on federal laws. For example, Native American tribes receive subsidies from the U.S. government as support for social programs, transportation, and education. There are scholarships expressly designated for Native Americans, and economic development is helped through the aid of federal tax-exemption schemes for private corporations or job-training facilities. Native Americans are also subject to both federal and state taxes.

Income sources vary from tribe to tribe. Many nations have built casinos to earn money that contributes to the tribe's finances. There are, however, other means through which tribes sustain themselves. These include special government programs, leasing, tourism, and compensations from treaty violations.

Major Crimes Act of 1885
A law that gave the United States government—instead of the individual tribal nations—authority over certain "serious" types of crimes.

Subsidies
Grants of money as a means of assistance. Often this money is given by the government to an individual, but it can also be granted from one body to another.

Manifest Destiny

Many white Americans in the 19th century believed it was their God-given right and duty to expand their territories westward to the Pacific and beyond. It was their manifest, or obvious, destiny.

Annexation

Taking over an area in order to incorporate it into a larger territory.

This idea was used by the U.S. government to justify campaigns against Native Americans and excuse the annexation of the territories of Oregon, Texas, California, and New Mexico in the 1840s and 1850s. It was later used to justify United States involvement in Cuba, the Dominican Republic, Hawaii, Alaska, and the Philippines.

The term was first used in 1845, when editor John L. O'Sullivan prophesied "the fulfillment of our manifest destiny to overspread the continent allotted by Providence…" in his *United States Magazine and Democratic Review*. In other words, America was a gift from God, and its control by white Americans was inevitable. Following O'Sullivan's article, politicians quickly picked up on the term.

The march of "progress"

O'Sullivan and other white Americans believed God gave America to them because they were the most advanced and civilized people in the world—in human history, in fact. Their spread into new lands therefore represented "progress."

Curriculum Context

Students should be able to describe the purpose, challenges, and economic incentives associated with westward expansion, including the concept of Manifest Destiny.

In turn, they believed that all Native Americans were inferior people with no right to the land under God's plan. Native Americans were exaggeratedly portrayed in newspapers—in both pictures and words—as violent savages who needed civilizing. This helped win white support for government campaigns against them.

Mestizos

The Mestizos were people with Spanish and Native American ancestry—*mestizo* is Spanish for "mixed race." Spanish men often had relationships with Native American women because few women accompanied the conquistadors of the 16th and 17th centuries on their trips to the Americas.

The men planned to pillage gold, silver, and other riches, not settle down and raise families. However, those men who did stay often took mistresses from among the local people. One of the first Mestizos was Martin, the son of Hernando Cortés, conqueror of Mexico, and his Native American interpreter, Malinche.

Mestizos were not fully accepted by either the Spanish or the Native Americans. To the Spanish they were racially inferior and could never attain the status of full-blooded Europeans. To Native Americans they were people who simply did not fit into the traditional way of life.

Unlike the Métis—their French and Native American counterparts in the North—the Mestizos did not form a distinct group. They tended to live on the margins of Native American society or were absorbed into the Spanish townships.

Curriculum Context

Explaining and evaluating Spanish interactions with Native American peoples will help students grasp the far reach of this powerful exploring nation.

Multiracial Americans

Eventually the Spanish brought Africans to the colonies as slaves. That meant there were three separate races, as well as the various mixes, living in the Americas. Children of Spanish and African parents were called Mulattos, and those born to Native Americans and Africans were called Zambos.

Métis

The Métis are a group of mixed-race people in Canada descended from late 17th-century Cree and French and Scottish fur trappers and traders—*métis* is French for "mixed race."

In the late 17th century trading companies such as the Hudson's Bay Company sent out fur trappers and traders to the unexplored areas of western North America. This was in response to the demands of the growing European middle class, which was beginning to develop a taste for luxury goods such as fur coats and hats. Over the next two centuries the demand for fur greatly increased—especially for beaver fur, which was used to adorn many fashionable clothes. As a result more and more trappers went out in search of beaver in areas such as Saskatchewan in Canada.

Luxury goods

Non-necessity goods, the demand for which increases with disposable income or wealth.

Friendly relations

Europeans thought Saskatchewan was uninhabited; but when the first trappers and traders arrived, they found Cree people had been living there for centuries. They offered the Cree goods in return for their help as guides and hunters. The whites and the Cree befriended each other, lived side by side, and shared the same rugged life.

Curriculum Context

Students may have need to describe the interaction of new settlers with already established Native Americans of the region.

Young Frenchmen were actively encouraged to marry Cree women in the belief that this would help spread French culture and expand opportunities for trade. Over the years many French and Scottish trappers married into the Cree and had children. These children, the first Métis, adopted aspects of both cultures: for example, they performed Native American religious rituals while also practicing the Catholic faith. They continued to work as fur trappers and traders, and often acted as interpreters for negotiations between Cree and Europeans.

At the end of the 18th century, when the British ousted the French and white settlements became more fully established, the status of the Métis declined. Not being fully Native Americans, they had no historical claims to owning land. Not being Europeans, they could not claim an automatic right to land. Some Métis were forced to leave their homes. The Métis tried to protect their land and trapping and trading rights in the two Riel Rebellions (1869–1870 and 1885) but were eventually defeated.

Curriculum Contex

In considering the struggle of groups of people caught between different cultural systems, students will better understand the Native American.

Staking their claim

The Métis have a major presence in Canada today, where their status has become an important political issue. For years the Métis have been ignored by successive governments while other Native American peoples have had their claims heard. Being of mixed-race descent, the Métis have had neither Native nor white American status. However, the number of societies battling for their rights and interests has grown considerably in recent years.

A statue of Louis Riel, leader of the Riel Rebellions, stands in front of the Manitoba Legislature, in Winnipeg, Manitoba.

RIEL

Missions

From the 1650s onward, European missionaries tried to convert Native Americans to Christianity, forcing many of them to live in settlements called missions. The effect on tribal identities and cultures was profound. Religion was at least partly involved when Europeans and Native Americans met, whether as friends or enemies. The missionaries felt it was their Christian duty and "educate" and "civilize" Native Americans, as well as convert them.

Counting the converted

Spain was a leader in missionary activity. Its armies of conquistadors were accompanied by Catholic priests who set up missions in Florida, the Southwest, and California. In Florida only Native Americans in missions were counted in population censuses as Spanish law decreed that only converted Native Americans had souls. In California many small native groups lost their separate identities and cultures when they were forced to live together in large Spanish missions.

Other European powers tried to convert Native Americans to their own particular Christian churches. French Jesuit missionaries, in competition with English Puritans, actively helped the French make trading links with Native Americans from their bases in Quebec. The Catholic Jesuits and Protestant Puritans both established settlements of converted Native Americans. The Puritans founded Quinnipiac reservation in New Haven in 1638, while the Jesuits founded Caughnawaga Mohawk Reservation in Quebec in 1676.

On the Northwest Coast, among the Inuit, Aleut, and Tlingit peoples of British Columbia and southern Alaska, the Russian Orthodox Church was granted a royal monopoly (exclusive control) in 1799. From there it spread its influence south to the Pomo peoples of California. Russian religious activity, like that of the

French, was linked with trade. This meant that Native Americans were converted not just to save their souls but also so they could be exploited as cheap labor.

Resistance to missions

In many cases there was Native American resistance to missionary activities. The Tlingit, for instance, rose against the Russian garrisons when the Russians took power away from their shamans. They gave in only when a fleet of Russian warships armed with cannons attacked their villages. In other cases there was little or no resistance. The Native Americans followed Christian rituals inside the mission churches but held traditional dances in the plazas outside.

Lasting influence

Many Pan-Indian movements were significantly influenced by Christianity. The Smohalla Cult, John Slocum's Indian Shaker Church, and Wovoka's Ghost Dance religion were all led by prophets who taught a combination of Christian and Native American beliefs.

In the 20th century, the last great Native American prophet, the Comanche leader Quanah Parker, helped found the most widespread Pan-Indian religion of today: the Native American Church. It uses peyote— a cactus that produces the drug mescal—for the sacrament and to induce hallucinations and visions. It combines this practice with Christian beliefs—taken from various branches of the Christian churches. About half of all Native Americans living in the U.S. today are members of the Native American Church.

The mission system started as a way of destroying Native American beliefs and replacing them with various forms of European Christianity. In the process it destroyed tribal cultures and identities. Today the Native American Church is a unifying force in reestablishing awareness of both.

Curriculum Context

Students may be asked to explain and evaluate the various strategies of Native Americans such as accommodation, revitalization, and resistance in some curricula.

Movies

Since the first days of film in the 1890s, Hollywood has made more Westerns than any other kind of movie. Even allowing for artistic license, almost all portray Native Americans inaccurately. This is because they were made by white people for a white audience and are set in a mythical past in which white heroes "won" the West.

Stereotypes

Fixed mental images, often about groups of people, that are based on oversimplified and untested thinking.

In most Westerns the immense cultural differences between Native Americans simply do not exist—they all live in tepees, wear feather headdresses, ride horses, and carry bows and arrows. They are also usually portrayed as one of three stereotypes: the Indian savage, who stands in the way of white civilization; the noble Indian, whose admirable but primitive way of life is doomed; and the Indian maiden, who usually falls in love with a white man and then dies tragically.

Origins of the stereotypes

As early as 1800, books and plays about Native Americans were more popular with white Americans than any other form of entertainment. In 1808 theater audiences were enthralled by *The Indian Princess*, the story of brave Pocahontas—the original Indian maiden. By 1840 there were more than 50 plays about her. The noble Indian originated in James Fenimore Cooper's frontier novels, such as *The Last of the Mohicans* (1826). Sentimental portraits of Native Americans from the past helped whites of the time avoid the problem of their own relations with Native Americans. Later, in the 1870s, Buffalo Bill Cody traveled with his successful Wild West show, called The Scouts of the Prairie, in which Native Americans were portrayed largely as Indian savages.

Novel entertainment

Audiences for the silent movies of the early 1900s wanted simple entertainment, so Native Americans were portrayed as they had been in books and plays. The Indian savage was still the most common stereotype, but the Indian maiden was quite popular, too. In *Kit Carson* (1903), native people murder a band of white trappers; a squaw helps the white hero, Kit, escape, but is killed for her good deed.

Not all of the hundreds of early movies about Native Americans portrayed them in such a stereotypical way. In *The Indian Land Grab* (1910), for example, a sophisticated white woman falls in love with a Native American man who is demanding land rights in Washington D.C., helps him win them, and then goes to live with him and his people. After 1912, when feature-length movies began to be made, exceptions to stereotypes continued. *The Silent Enemy* (1930), was a realistic portrayal of the Ojibway's (Chippewa's) struggle to avoid starvation in the days before settlers—but it was a commercial failure.

Curriculum Context

Some curricula ask students to distinguish between unsupported expressions of opinion and informed hypotheses grounded in historical evidence.

Buffalo Bill Cody's Wild West Show featured both Buffalo Bill and Sitting Bull, seen here in 1885.

Double take

Stars were signed to make several movies a year, and it was common to shoot two movies at once, and use the same action footage. Not surprisingly, the Indian savage was the main stereotype in these movies—as it was in the big feature

Westerns of the time. Epics such as *The Covered Wagon* (1934), *Stagecoach* (1939), and *Western Union* (1941) told of the triumph of white civilization over Indian savages and the wilderness.

The 1930s and 1940s in particular were eras of low-budget, action-packed Westerns, produced by the big studios. The Indian maiden was the least used stereotype of this era, but the noble Indian commonly appeared as the white hero's loyal helper. Tonto, faithful companion of the Lone Ranger, features in several low-budget movies. Stereotypes persisted, but moviemakers became more aware of how white Americans have distorted the history of the West. In *Fort Apache* (1948) actor Henry Fonda plays an arrogant, racist fort commander whose refusal to negotiate with Cochise results in the massacre of his own troops. In *Broken Arrow* (1950) James Stewart stars as a man who studies Apache culture so that he can talk peace with Cochise. The Apache leader is portrayed as a man of honor and the movie's hero by refusing to break the negotiated treaty.

Curriculum Context

Students might find it useful to look for examples of movies or books that acknowledge the distortion of Western history in popular culture.

Era of the doomed Indian

After *Broken Arrow* the noble Indian in the form of the doomed hero became the dominant stereotype. *Crazy Horse* (1953), *Sitting Bull* (1954), and *Geronimo* (1962) all treat their subjects sympathetically in this way. In some movies, such as *The Searchers* (1956), *Major Dundee* (1964), and *Ulzana's Raid* (1972), the Indian savage is used only to illustrate white savagery.

The early 1970s saw various attempts by white moviemakers to portray Native Americans authentically, but with limited success. *A Man Called Horse* (1970), for example, accurately portrays some aspects of Sioux culture, such as their homes, but misrepresents others—notably the Sun Dance, which it shows as a barbaric test of bravery, not a sacred rite. After the mid-1970s traditional Westerns lost their box-office appeal. In those that have been made since, such as *Dances with Wolves* (1990), the Indian savage has vanished, but the noble Indian and the Indian maiden persist.

A few mainstream movies since 1975 have tried to deal authentically with Native American life today. *Three Warriors* (1977), for example, deals with the struggles of young Native Americans to reconcile traditional and modern ways of life. On the whole, mainstream movies have avoided authentic portrayals of Native American life because they are usually commercial failures.

Mainstream
The generally accepted thoughts or trends of the majority population.

More say in the matter
In the early days of cinema, Native American actors were usually restricted to playing extras, with white stars playing Native American speaking parts. Even in recent times Native American roles have sometimes been given to non-Native Americans: in *Flap* (1970), for example, the non-Native American actor Anthony Quinn plays the leading Native American role.

Since the late 1960s, however, Native Americans have become more involved in determining their on-screen roles. In 1966 Jay Silverheels founded the Indian Actors Workshop and the Indian Actors Guild to teach acting to Native Americans and promote their use in Native American roles. In 1972 Kiowa author N. Scott Momaday's 1968 Pulitzer-Prize-winning novel *House Made of Dawn* was made into a movie, with a script written by him and with Native American actors. Native Americans therefore have much more say in how they are portrayed in movies.

Curriculum Context

Various curricula ask students to recognize that people from different cultures develop different ways of interpreting experience.

Pan-Indian Movement

The Pan-Indian Movement is a term that describes Native American political activism that is guided by the idea of "Indianness" or being "Indian." This idea comes from the common experience of being Native American, which is shared by people of Native American descent who have a similar history and have been treated in a similar way by the U.S. authorities.

Curriculum Context

Students may be asked to consider how individual contributions affected the broader Native American society.

Segregation

The act of keeping separate; in regard to people, segregation can call for divisions along racial, cultural, or other lines, some of which may be arbitrary.

The term Pan-Indian Movement uses the Greek word "pan"—which means "all." The groups that have been called Pan-Indian are mainly those that have worked for the combined interests of all Native Americans and whose interests echo those of the majority of Native Americans. However, the term does not exclude local groups that—although they act within the boundaries of their tribal nation—have indirectly managed to achieve things for all Native Americans. Such groups have awakened the interest of other Americans in important social and political issues.

Segregation and integration

At the beginning of the 20th century, Native Americans began to work together to get their rights recognized. The painful experience of the past century had made them realize that they could achieve more by acting together. At the time this idea tied in with the U.S. government's policy of integration, which argued that Native Americans should leave behind their old traditions in order to become modern U.S. citizens.

The Society of American Indians (SAI) was formed in 1911 from this idea. At that time it was generally believed that the small numbers of Native Americans living in the United States would survive only if they were fully integrated into Anglo-American society. Many Native Americans believed that survival meant giving up their old ways and accepting the U.S. way of life.

The SAI had been funded by Native Americans who came from the Carlisle Indian School in Pennsylvania. Among them were Arthur Parker (Seneca), Francis La Flesche (Omaha), Carlos Montezuma (Apache), and Marie Baldwin (Ojibway/Chippewa). They believed it was important for Native Americans to have the same rights as other Americans. At the time Native Americans were not citizens of the United States, had no right to vote, and had little control over government legislation that affected their lives. The SAI gained many supporters, but the group met with opposition from other Native Americans who felt it was essential to emphasize that they were culturally different from other Americans.

In 1924 the SAI succeeded in its campaign for U.S. citizenship to be granted to all Native Americans. However, in 1944 a new organization called the National Congress of American Indians (NCAI) was created that opposed the SAI. This new group strongly supported the interests of the Native Americans who wished to retain their traditional culture.

A new approach
The NCAI spoke in terms of "Indian culture" and "Indian people." This approach was more popular than talking about the "Indian race," which was the theme that united the SAI. Native American culture was more important than tribal differences and gave all Native Americans a common identity. Adopting this approach, the NCAI succeeded where the SAI had failed.

In 1961 Chicago hosted the American Indian Chicago Conference. Many representatives from different peoples came together to discuss common plans for a Pan-Indian future. Following the formation of the NCAI, other associations started up in the 1960s. They were the National Indian Youth Council (NIYC) and the more confrontational American Indian Movement (AIM).

Time for Protest

The 1960s and 1970s were crucial in the development of ideas related to Pan-Indianism. Native American protest groups had a similar approach to that of African-American organizations that were fighting for their own civil rights. Native American priorities included treaty recognition, tribal sovereignty, land rights, and rights of cultural and religious expression. Other major issues were unemployment, poverty, and discrimination.

AIM was an extremely politically active organization. It was involved in historical events such as the occupation of Alcatraz Island in San Francisco Bay in 1969 and the Trail of Broken Treaties Caravan in 1972, when the offices of the Bureau of Indian Affairs were occupied during a march to Washington.

In 1973 the 71-day siege of Wounded Knee II brought AIM to the attention of the world's media. It started when the Lakota, supported by AIM, protested about local corruption by occupying the site of Wounded Knee, where many Sioux had been massacred in 1890. The occupation attracted people from other groups protesting about Native American rights in general. During the siege two AIM members were killed by federal agents.

This episode marked a very important moment in Native American history—it still holds deep significance for Native Americans because it told the world of their suffering and poverty. The events of Wounded Knee II marked a new era in Pan-Indian activism.

Worldwide connections

People arrested during and after the events of Wounded Knee II were considered by AIM to be political prisoners. Some, like Leonard Peltier, a Sioux

Occupation

The act of seizing and controlling land, usually by military force.

Political prisoners

Persons who are imprisoned for involvement in political activities.

incarcerated for killing two FBI agents in a shootout at Pine Ridge Indian Reservation, are still in jail. Amnesty International, the international association for political and human rights, has raised concerns about the fairness of his case.

After these events the Native Americans' fight to have their rights recognized received more attention. For example, in 1974 the International Indian Treaty Council (IITC), along with several other groups from all over the world, was recognized in Geneva, Switzerland, as one of the nongovernmental organizations that defended the rights of native peoples.

Curriculum Context

Many curricula encourage students to identify reasons for and the impact of incidents of civil protest.

Native North Americans have now established a network with other native peoples of the world, such as Australian Aborigines, New Zealand Maori, and other minority peoples in South and Central America. These are important contacts that emphasize the political importance of Pan-Indian movements and bring their issues to an international audience.

Cooperation with other native peoples also helps attract the attention of development agencies and international human rights support groups. These groups, in turn, play an important part in the process of achieving recognition for Native American human and legal rights.

Red Power

Similar approaches between African-American and Native American protest groups led militant Native American groups to use the term "Red Power"—modeled after the African-American "Black Power."

Pueblo Rebellion

Francisco Vasquez de Coronado led an expedition north from Mexico into the territory of the present-day United States in 1540–1542. But the first large-scale attempt by the Spanish to settle in what is now New Mexico and Texas did not begin for another 56 years. In 1598–1599 the Spanish explorer Juan de Oñate conquered the Pueblo peoples of the Rio Grande valley and began a long period of tyrannical Spanish rule.

The Pueblo were treated like slaves and forced to hand over food and other goods to the Spanish. The Spanish also built churches, and their missionaries tried to convert Native Americans to Christianity and prevent them from following their traditional religions.

The Pueblo had previously traded some of their corn with the Apache, but because the Spanish stopped this trade, the Apache began attacking both the Pueblo and the Spaniards ever more fiercely.

Diseases brought by the Spanish and a long drought in the 1660s combined to create enormous misery for the Pueblo. Their population fell from about 70,000 people when Oñate arrived to about 17,000 in 1680. By then the Pueblo could bear their oppression no longer and rose in rebellion.

Resistance to Spain

The rebellion was inspired by Popé, a religious leader of the Tewa people from San Juan (New Mexico). The Spanish publicly whipped Popé on several occasions because he continued to practice his religion. Because of this humiliation Popé journeyed from village to village persuading the leaders of each to join in the revolt.

Then, in August 1680, the Pueblo attacked. Popé and his followers destroyed many churches and killed the priests

and any other Spaniards they could find. Next, they besieged the main Spanish town of Santa Fe, captured it, and forced the Spanish governor and his people to flee to El Paso, Texas. About 400 Spaniards died during the fighting.

The ruins of an ancient Pueblo site in Chaco Canyon, New Mexico.

Popé ruled a number of villages of his Tewa people from then until his death in 1688 or 1690. He was a cruel chief, however, and his tyranny wrecked the unity of the Pueblo peoples that he had created at the start of the rebellion. The Apache, some of whom had helped in the rebellion, also stepped up their attacks on the villages. These attacks made some of the Pueblo believe that Spanish "protection" was not such a bad thing after all.

The Spaniards fight back

Taking advantage of the situation, a new Spanish governor, Diego de Vargas, began reestablishing Spanish rule in 1692. In 1693 Vargas recaptured Santa Fe, and after a further five years of cruel fighting he conquered almost all of the Pueblo once again. Only the Hopi people remained independent, probably because the Spanish found it so difficult to attack their remote settlements.

Quivira

Spanish explorers of the 16th century believed that a city rich in gold and jewels that they called "Quivira" existed in what is now Arizona and New Mexico. This imaginary city was only one of the fabled Seven Cities of Gold that the explorers believed could be found in the new country.

Curriculum Context

Many curricula challenge students to analyze the motivation and ambition of European explorers.

Francisco Vasquez de Coronado was the most famous of the Spaniards to search for Quivira. In 1539 he was in Mexico when he received a report from a Spanish friar that mentioned the northern cities of gold. In 1540 Coronado set out into the area north of the Rio Grande to look for the cities, but all he found were Zuni adobe villages. He kept looking for his goal, but all the Native Americans he met deliberately misled him because he had not come as their friend.

The Zuni told him about Tusayan, another legendary city. Coronado went where he was directed but again found only Hopi adobe villages. The Hopi told Coronado he would find wealth at Tiguex, which is today an abandoned pueblo. Again, he found only adobe villages.

Coronado sent out exploratory parties in several directions from Tiguex. They found no gold and, returning to Tiguex, discovered the people had deserted the pueblo. But one of his expeditionary forces reported from Pecos—another then-abandoned pueblo—that Quivira lay to the east in the area that is now Kansas. With 30 men Coronado set off in 1541 for Quivira. He found instead the grass-thatched lodges of the Wichita. Infuriated, he forced a Wichita guide to take him back to Mexico. The guide, aware of the tricks played on Coronado by the Hopi and Zuni, led him in circles. The Wichita set an ambush, and Coronado's lieutenant, Juan de Padillo, was killed.

Railroads

In the 19th century the building of the railroad system had an enormous impact on North America. It proved financially beneficial for the white population but was detrimental to the Native Americans, especially to those groups who lived on the Great Plains.

The U.S. railroad first developed in the East in the 1830s. By the 1850s, New England and the mid-Atlantic states had 9,000 miles (14,400 km) of railroad tracks. Based on the success of these lines, the railroad companies decided to expand the tracks westward. They envisioned a railroad line that would connect the East and West coasts.

In 1862 the U.S. government approved construction of the Union Pacific and Central Pacific railroad lines to create an East–West route. The Union Pacific would run west from Iowa and the Central Pacific east from Sacramento, California. In 1869 the two railroad lines met at Promontory, Utah. By 1883 three more transcontinental railroad lines had been built: the Atlantic and Pacific, Southern Pacific, and Northern Pacific. Many railroad tracks cut through the Great Plains, home to many Native American peoples.

Following the buffalo

All Plains groups depended on the buffalo herds that roamed the Plains for food, clothing, and shelter. The building of railroad lines drastically disrupted the migratory patterns of the buffalo. The railroad building crews cut across the landscape, creating physical barriers that the buffalo could not cross. The herds, unable to roam as before, were unable to breed. The railroads further disturbed the buffalo lands by encouraging cattle drives across the Plains. Ranchers used the drives to move their cattle to railheads serving the East.

Curriculum Context

Many curricula ask students to describe the purpose, challenges, and events associated with westward expansion.

Migratory patterns

Movements from one place to another that are often associated with the seasons, feeding, or breeding.

Curriculum Context

Some students will want to examine the impact of economic developments and westward territorial expansion on relations with Native Americans.

A way of life ends

The near destruction of the buffalo was fatal for the Plains peoples, who had no other source of food. The government hastened their demise by giving land that had been taken from the Plains peoples to workers on the railroad crews. Men who had worked on the railroad were given special grants of land on which they were allowed to settle.

Without food and with their lands reduced in size, the Plains peoples grew too weak to withstand the government pressure to move onto reservations. The railroads had destroyed the migratory hunting life on which they depended.

The Union Pacific–Central Pacific railroad ran for 1,780 miles (2,860 km) of track. The construction of the four transcontinental railroads was a huge feat of engineering and employed thousands of workers over decades.

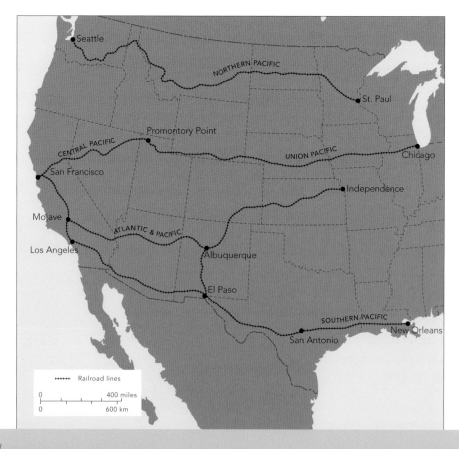

Recognition

For the United States government the term *recognition* means the official acceptance of a group of Native Americans as a tribe. Once recognized by the federal government, a tribe is able to manage its own affairs largely free from government interference and is considered an independent nation in matters relating to tribal interests.

Federal recognition is straightforward in practice, but it is prone to legal arguments and courtroom disputes. The reason for this is that the government's definition of a tribe is often very different from most Native Americans' idea of a tribe.

Defining a tribe

The Native American view is that if a group of people lives together as a unified community that shares common beliefs, ideas, and customs derived from native tradition, then that community is a tribe.

Defining a tribe member varies from tribe to tribe. Some tribes rely solely on the amount of Native American ancestry in someone's family to determine membership. Others might permit a person who has been adopted by members of the tribe or who has married into the community to be considered as a tribal member, provided the new member plays an active role in community affairs and concerns.

The federal government, however, requires certain criteria for tribal recognition that make it difficult for some Native American communities to qualify. For example, the federal government asks for historical evidence that the group has functioned as a community since the time the community first made contact with Europeans. Since Native Americans did not keep the type of records the government requires

Ancestry

A person's lineage or group descent.

Curriculum Context

The goal of some curricula may be to have students explore relationships between culture and governmental policy.

as evidence, meeting the criteria often means using the accounts written by the European explorers who first encountered the native peoples. Some of these reports are biased, others are factually incorrect, and nearly all of them fail to understand the subtle details of native communal life and the cultural ties that bound the tribal people together.

The government also requires that the community be named on treaty agreements that have been approved by Congress and that it has continually occupied a single territory over a long period of time. However, many Native American groups were nomadic, moving from one camp to another throughout the year, and this makes it difficult to prove they have occupied a single territory. Others have migrated or been forced to move from their original homelands.

By the 19th century many tribes had had their numbers reduced through wars and epidemics, forcing them to join with other, larger groups to survive. Most treaties

Nomadic

Having no permanent home and moving from one place to another according to the seasons in search of hunting grounds, water, and grazing land.

Case study on recognition

The difficulties of gaining recognition are highlighted by the case of the Mashpee, a Wampanoag tribal community living on Cape Cod, Massachusetts. In 1976 the Mashpee sued the federal government for the return of 16,000 acres (6,475 ha) of land and, in the process, had to prove they were a tribe. The town of Mashpee was governed solely by Native Americans until 1964, but according to the government's policy of integration and assimilation, the people living there had adopted some nonnative values. Although they had the support of anthropologists

from the Smithsonian Institution, the Mashpee lost their case because they had become too Westernized when they followed the government's earlier policies. They were considered to have broken their native traditions and disqualified themselves from gaining official tribal status.

Some groups, such as the Lumbee in North Carolina, have gained state but not federal recognition and are considered as tribes only within their own state.

between the U.S. government and Native American groups were negotiated during the 19th century, and some of these treaties applied only to the larger tribes, neglecting the smaller communities that might have been living with the larger ones.

Benefits of recognition

Despite these federal obstacles, it is important for tribal communities to obtain official recognition. As recognized tribes, they become eligible for federal aid and federally funded projects, without which the community might be unable to survive. The official status also serves to establish an identity for the group that is socially important.

Reexamining the law

Until recently, tribes that failed to gain recognition through the courts had little possibility of having the rulings overturned unless they could provide new evidence. However, in 1991 the government introduced new rules for recognition under which appeals against court decisions could be made to a division of the Federal Acknowledgment and Research Project.

Despite this change, many tribal communities remain uncertain about their official status, and therefore the new rules are in the process of being revised again. The Native Americans' argument is a simple one. They believe that the issue of recognition must be decided using native criteria for determining which communities can be called tribes, instead of relying on the nonnative historical documents the federal government has insisted on so far.

Curriculum Context

For some curricula, students are asked to describe the internecine Indian conflicts, including the competing claims for control of lands, and the results of those conflicts.

Federal Acknowledgment and Research Project

An office established to review claims in regard to the government's recognition of a tribal community.

Reservations

Native American reservations in North America are lands that have been reserved—or set aside—for the exclusive use of the Native Americans living on them. Reservations were first established in the 18th century by means of formal written agreements made between European colonists in North America and different Native American groups.

Curriculum Context

Students should recognize how European groups viewed the cultures they encountered in the course of their explorations and settlements.

Sovereign nations

The Europeans wanted to formally divide up land and say in a way that was legally binding that certain North American lands belonged to them and that other lands belonged to the tribes. The colonists who made these first agreements treated the Native American groups as sovereign nations—groups of people who made their own laws and decisions about who lived on their land and what customs were followed there.

The reservations were intended to protect both Native Americans and the Europeans. They set clear boundaries beyond which neither had the right to interfere with the other. Colonists were not allowed to settle in the reservations, and the Native Americans

An aerial view of a Lakota camp probably on or near Pine Ridge Reservation, South Dakota.

agreed that they would not prevent colonists settling outside the Native American areas. Problems began when the European populations grew, and more land was needed to house the increased numbers of people. The only land available was Native American land.

The early treaties did, however, at least establish the right of Native Americans to occupy lands they had inherited from previous generations. They believed these lands were important to them because they included traditional hunting and fishing grounds and because they were holy places where their ancestors were buried.

In 1763 British colonists established the Proclamation Line. This stated that lands east of the line could be settled on by Europeans, while lands west of the Mississippi were for Native American use.

Creating the United States
The American Revolution of 1776 changed this position completely. The United States became an independent, sovereign nation, and agreements made by British colonists were seen by the new Americans as nothing more than the law of a foreign power to be discarded at will. After 1776, therefore, lands west of the Mississippi were considered lands on which Americans could legally settle. Native Americans were living on these lands, however, and treaties were now made by the new Americans that limited Native American lands to an even greater extent than before 1776. This was the start of the modern reservations.

Between 1778 and 1871, when the policy was ended, a total of 389 treaties had been signed and ratified. Many eastern peoples were removed from their traditional homelands and resettled in the Indian Territory west of the Mississippi. Although this was within the area the British had defined with the

Proclamation Line

An imaginary boundary line running through North America from Canada to Florida. Established in 1763, the line was supposed to separate lands meant for Native American use from those held for the colonists.

Curriculum Context

Students studying the federal Indian policy after the American Revolution should evaluate the long-term effects on the relationship between Native Americans and the U.S. government.

Proclamation Line, it was much smaller and later became the state of Oklahoma.

Outside Oklahoma reservations were set aside for Native Americans to ensure that whites had an undisputed claim to the lands where they settled. Most Native Americans had little choice in these agreements. They had already been subdued by military conquest, and the reservations seemed at least to provide a way of keeping what little land they had remaining to them. They were also under pressure to conform to a dominant white society, and the reservation agreements ensured they would have access to white education and medical facilities, as well as housing and food supplies. These provisions, called annuities, were guaranteed by the government.

The old arrangement of making treaties between sovereign nations was kept so that modern reservations still have their own governments, or tribal councils, that are responsible for any legal matters affecting the reservation. They also retain rights to minerals, timber, and other resources within the reservation areas.

Because these agreements were made with the federal government, or with the British Crown in Canada, most reservations remain outside any laws passed by local states and provinces. They are subject to federal or Canadian central government control, which is administered through the Bureau of Indian Affairs, but reservations are allowed to set their own laws and taxes within their borders.

Curriculum Context

Some curricula will ask students to analyze political issues such as Indian policies, the growth of political machines, and civil service reform.

Modern reservations
There were about 310 federally recognized reservations in the United States in 2005. Most of these had been set up under the federal system and are known today as federal reservations, but a number have also been

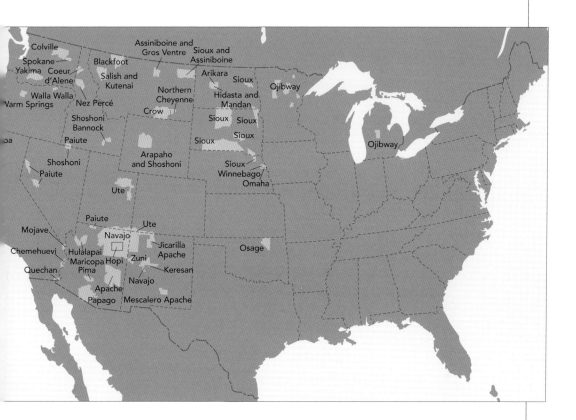

Colville
Spokane
Yakima Coeur
d'Alene
Walla Walla
Varm Springs
Blackfoot
Salish and
Kutenai
Nez Percé
Shoshoni
Bannock
Paiute
Shoshoni
Paiute
Ute
Assiniboine and
Gros Ventre
Sioux and
Assiniboine
Northern
Cheyenne
Crow
Arikara
Sioux
Hidasta and
Mandan
Sioux Sioux
Sioux
Sioux
Arapaho
and Shoshoni
Sioux
Winnebago
Omaha
Ojibway
Ojibway
oa
Paiute
Mojave
Chemehuevi Hulalapai
Maricopa Pima
Quechan
Apache
Papago
Ute
Navajo
Zuni
Jicarilla
Apache
Hopi
Keresan
Navajo
Mescalero Apache
Osage

established by U.S. states. Those set up by states are subject to state authority and have less independence than federal reservations. They are, for example, subject to state taxes. In addition, there are several reservations that are not recognized by any U.S. authority. These are mainly located in the East and in California, where reservations were created before the federal system.

Reservation areas

The Navajo reservation in New Mexico, Arizona, Colorado, and Utah is the largest in the United States, with a population of more than 200,000, although the combined Chippewa–Ojibway reservations in Canada and the United States are larger still. The Pima–Papago also have large reservations in the Southwest, covering an area of 2.4 million acres (1 million ha). The smallest reservation, a grave site in central California, is only 32 square feet (3 sq. m) in area.

The largest of the modern Native American U.S. reservations are shown as yellow areas on this map. It can be seen how far west of the Mississippi they all lie and what a small proportion of the total land area Native Americans can now call their own.

Riel Rebellions

Louis Riel was a Métis—someone of mixed French and Native American origin—who became important in 1869 because of his attempts to have Métis status officially recognized in Canada.

When Canada became a self-governing dominion of the British empire in 1867, the new prime minister, John Macdonald, encouraged expansion by white settlers. This threatened the traditional hunting and trading way of life of the Métis. Lead by Louis Riel, they rebelled and demanded legal representation in the Canadian parliament. After several inconclusive confrontations, the Métis were officially recognized by the Canadian government, granted the province of Manitoba, and allowed to form their own government with limited autonomy. They elected Riel as their president.

Opposition in parliament to Métis demands meant they had little real say in matters that affected them. Threats against Riel's life drove him into exile in Montana, while white settlers and whiskey dealers invaded Manitoba illegally, forcing the Métis to move to Saskatchewan.

Cree join second revolt

Riel began a second rebellion in 1884, this time with support from other Native American groups, especially the Cree. The Métis and their Native American allies won all the early battles but were finally defeated. Riel was taken prisoner and tried for treason.

The court found Riel guilty and sentenced him to death. Supporters begged him to save his own life by pleading insanity. He refused and was hanged on November 16, 1885.

Parliament

The highest legislative body of various nations, including Canada.

Curriculum Context

Students may find it useful to examine the influence and achievements of significant leaders of various Native American groups.

Russia, Wars with

Alaska was governed by Russia from the mid-18th century until 1867, when the territory was sold to the United States. Throughout this time the Russians, like other European colonials, ruthlessly exploited the Native Americans in the region. As a result there were many violent clashes between the Russians and the native people.

Early Russian trading posts

Russian involvement in Alaska began with the Danish explorer Vitus Bering, who was hired in 1728 by the Russian government to explore the area now known as the Bering Sea. In 1741 Bering died in the territory while leading an expedition. Some of his men returned to Russia with valuable sea-otter furs. Other Russian fur trappers soon began visiting the Aleutian Islands, and in 1784 they founded a colony on Kodiak Island. These first Russian visitors to Alaska were tough men. Many of them had been sent to work there as punishment for crimes they had committed.

During much of the late 18th century the method that the Russians used to obtain furs was to raid a village, take hostage the women and children, and force the men out of the village to trap animals. If the village men did not return with the right number of pelts, then Russians would kill the women and children.

In the early 1760s the Aleut and Inuit began to rebel. Off the island of Kamchatka the Aleut destroyed five Russian trading ships in 1761. Such raids continued until 1766, when Ivan Soloviev led a group of naval ships that attacked Aleut village after village, killing men, women, and children. Soloviev was successful in ending the Aleut rebellion and in the process nearly wiped out the whole tribe.

Curriculum Context

In many curricula, students are asked to identify the goals, obstacles, and accomplishments of key European expeditions.

Pelts

Animal skins with the hair or fur attached.

These children are Aleuts, one of the Native American groups found in Alaska. Theirs was one of the groups to come into contact with Russian explorers and fur traders in the 1700s.

Tlingit resistance

In 1799 the Russian government put a trading business called the Russian American Company in charge of Alaska and the Kurile Islands. The chief manager of the company was Aleksandr Baranov, who was effectively the first governor of Alaska. He reorganized the fur trapping and trading operations, but was cruel in his dealings with native peoples. Baranov built a new trading post in southern Alaska named St. Michael in 1799 and set up other settlements on the Alaskan mainland. However, he did not succeed in subduing the local Tlingit tribe.

In the late 1790s the Tlingit refused to trade with the Russians, claiming that Russian goods were more expensive and of poorer quality than British or American goods. The Tlingit also resented Russian advances into their territory. They began raiding the settlements, wiping out Glory of Russia (near present-day Yakutat) and, in 1802, destroying St. Michael. The Russians sent a full-scale military expedition to retake the post in 1804 and renamed it New Archangel. The Russians left in 1867 but never subdued the Tlingit.

Mainland

The primary part of a land mass or continent.

Curriculum Context

Many curricula ask students to study the causes and consequences of the violent conflicts between European settlers and Native Americans as nations struggled for control of North America.

Sand Creek Massacre

The Sand Creek Massacre occurred on November 29, 1864. It was one of the most brutal events of the long struggle between white settlers and Native Americans. At this time, white settlers and prospectors were moving into the Colorado territory to search for gold. To make way for the increase in white settlers, the government needed land.

The land in the area belonged to the Cheyenne and Arapaho. They refused when the government tried to persuade them to relocate to reservations.

In the spring of 1864, settlers and native warriors had minor clashes in Colorado. In retaliation the Cheyenne and Arapaho raided wagon trails leading into Colorado. The territorial government then raised a militia under the command of Colonel John Chivington.

At this point Chief Black Kettle of the Southern Cheyenne and other tribal leaders persuaded their people to accept a peace offer that the territorial governor, John Evans, had proposed. Evans promised Black Kettle that, if he set up camp near Fort Lyon, his people would not be attacked.

The massacre

However, at dawn on November 29, Chivington surrounded Black Kettle's camp. Black Kettle raised both a white flag and the U.S. flag to show his peaceful intentions. Chivington ignored the flags and ordered his troops to attack. More than 200 Cheyenne, mostly women and children, were murdered in the onslaught.

The angry Cheyenne and Arapaho warriors continued attacking wagon trails and army posts until 1865, when the government condemned Chivington's attack and negotiated new treaties.

Curriculum Context

Any study of history is likely to ask students to explain the significance of the actions of certain key individuals.

Onslaught

An overwhelming force; the word *onslaught* is often used in reference to an overwhelming violent force or devastating attack.

Seminole Wars

During the War of 1812 the Seminole sided with the British against the Americans. At the time the Seminole further angered the U.S. government by harboring escaped African-American slaves (called "Freedmen"). Since Florida was then a Spanish colony, and Spanish–Seminole relations were very good, it was difficult for slaveowners to reclaim their slaves.

Armed clashes with the Seminole in 1816 and 1817 led the United States to plan a full-scale attack against the tribe. An invasion of Florida began in March 1818 under General Andrew Jackson. Jackson's troops destroyed many Seminole villages and captured the Spanish capital at Pensacola in May. Spain had few resources to oppose this attack and began talks with the U.S. government. The resulting Adams–Onís Treaty of 1819 made Florida part of the United States and therefore a region where slave-owning was legal. After Jackson's attacks most Seminole and Red Stick Creek were forced to move to the swampy lakeland areas of northern Florida and near modern Orlando and Tampa.

The fight against removal
White settlers flooded in to Florida through the 1820s, and as a result many Creek were forced to move from Florida to the Indian Territory (now Oklahoma). In the early 1830s, a few remaining Seminole leaders reluctantly signed the Treaty of Paynes Landing (1832), which stated that the tribe should move to the Indian Territory within three years. The treaty was soon rejected by the Seminole as a whole.

Chief Osceola now emerged as the main Seminole leader. Faced with the threat of removal, Osceola led a rebellion in November 1835 by killing another Seminole leader who had agreed to move to the Indian Territory. This signaled the start of the Second Seminole War.

Curriculum Context

Many curricula ask students to explain the influence of leaders of a particular time.

Osceola and other chiefs launched a series of raids on U.S. Army forts and white settlements. During the years of bitter fighting that followed, the Seminole made good use of their knowledge of how to survive in the swamplands. Using guerrilla tactics, they repeatedly outwitted American troops who tried to hunt them down.

Osceola was captured after attending fake peace talks. He died in jail in South Carolina in early 1838. In December 1837 U.S. forces under General Zachary Taylor won a major battle at Lake Okeechobee, during which many Seminole were killed.

Removal and peace at last

Over the next few years several thousand Seminole moved to the Indian Territory, but armed clashes continued until 1842. In that year the United States gave up trying to pry the Seminole from their last strongholds deep in the Everglades. From 1855 to 1858, the tribe fought the Third Seminole War to try to stop further white incursions into their territory. After this final confrontation, only about 200 Seminole opted to remain in Florida.

Guerrilla Tactics
Military techniques by which small bands of warriors, often indigenous people, carry out a campaign of harrassment against the enemy.

In this painting, created in around 1835, Seminole Indians attack a fort on the Withlacoochee River, Florida.

Settlers

The relationship between Native Americans and settlers was a complex one, and there were many misunderstandings on both sides. In general Native Americans could not understand the settlers' wish to own the lands they lived on. For their part the settlers could not understand the Native American belief that land was sacred and could not be the property of any one individual.

Curriculum Context

Students will find it helpful to compare and contrast the exploration and settlement motivations of some of the European nations.

Navigational aids

Instruments and information to help sailors get from one place to another on the open water.

The early settlers came primarily from four different European nations—Spain, France, England, and the Netherlands. Groups from each country had their own reasons for wishing to settle in North America. Each adopted a different policy toward the Native Americans whom they encountered.

Each of the European nations that sent settlers to North America was driven by a strong desire for exploration. They were aided in this by technological advances, such as better navigational aids. In 1492 the explorer Christopher Columbus had suggested the New World had a wealth of economic resources for Europeans to exploit. Many settlers also wished to escape from religious conflicts between Protestants and Catholics in their own countries.

Colonizing North America

The first European settlement in North America was St. Augustine in Florida, which the Spanish built in 1565. The Spanish also explored the Southwest and established Santa Fe in New Mexico in 1609.

Meanwhile, England was forming its own colonies. Jamestown in Virginia was founded in 1607, and the Pilgrims arrived in Massachusetts in 1620. Dutch and French interests were centered on the economic benefits of the fur trade rather than on permanent settlements. However, they both also formed fairly large communities in New York (Dutch—originally "New Amsterdam") and Canada (French).

Most of the early settlers cooperated with the Native Americans they came into contact with. Indeed, Jamestown survived its early years only because the colonists there received some support from a confederacy of tribes called the Powhatan. French interests were also served by friendly contacts, including marriages between French and Native Americans.

Curriculum Context

Students might be asked to describe ways in which Native Americans cooperated with settlers, such as in the fur trade.

These early friendships quickly deteriorated when Europeans, particularly the English, demanded Native American lands for their plantations. The colony of Virginia, which had come to rely on tobacco-growing after Sir Walter Raleigh introduced tobacco to Europe, wanted room for growing the crop. Conflicts arose both between the settlers and Native Americans and between the different European powers.

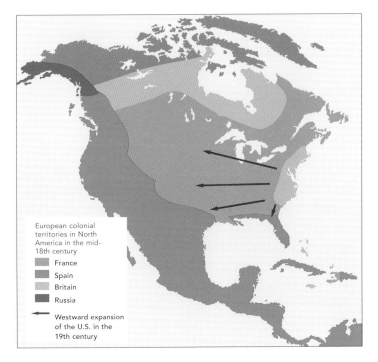

European colonial territories in North America in the mid-18th century

France

Spain

Britain

Russia

← Westward expansion of the U.S. in the 19th century

European settlers began colonizing North America in the early 16th century. This map illustrates the European territorial claims to North America until the mid-18th century and later the expansion of U.S. settlers across the continent.

An attempt at compromise

To avoid conflict and keep the Native Americans and the settlers apart, Great Britain declared the Proclamation Line in 1763. It was intended to make land west of the Mississippi an area for Native Americans where white settlement was forbidden, leaving the eastern regions for Europeans. However, the Proclamation Line lasted only a short time and was ignored after the American Revolution of 1776.

The newly formed U.S. government tried to resolve these issues by making treaties with the tribes. These treaties meant that tribes gave up many of their rights and allowed settlement outside areas previously occupied by colonists. Many groups signed away lands in return for benefits they never received.

The U.S. government realized there would be conflict between Native Americans living in the treaty areas and settlers who wished to claim these lands. The Indian Removal Act of the 1830s enabled the United States to forcibly remove tribes from their original homelands if these were wanted for settlement. Many of the disputes between Native Americans and the United States that continue today stem from this policy of treating Native Americans as people without rights to territories they originally occupied.

Dividing up the land

Matters came to a head in 1862 with the Homestead Act, which opened up Native American lands in Kansas and Nebraska to white settlement. The Allotment Act of 1887 was an attempt to break up the reservations. It gave each Native American family 160 acres (65 ha) of land but took away any tribal control. However, this was too small an area for Native Americans who depended on hunting for survival.

Spain, Wars with

After Christopher Columbus landed in America in 1492, Spanish conquistadors began colonizing islands in the Caribbean. Within 30 years they had moved on to the North American mainland and subdued the powerful Aztec rulers of Mexico. By the late 16th century, the Spanish empire had spread to include much of present-day Arizona, New Mexico, Texas, and Florida.

The Spanish also made ruthless use of their superior military technology. Native Americans had no firearms and no knowledge of metalwork to compete with the Spaniards' swords and body armor. Horses were also a new and terrifying sight for Native Americans. With these advantages a few hundred Spaniards defeated native armies that numbered many thousands of warriors.

The first large-scale conquest began when Hernando Cortés led an expedition to Mexico in 1519. The Aztec ruler Montezuma II led a huge, powerful, and warlike empire, but it seems he believed Cortés was an incarnation of an Aztec god and did little to hinder his advance. Cortés was quickly established in the Aztec capital of Tenochtitlán (now Mexico City) but had to leave soon after to defeat a Spanish rival. When he returned, he had to mount a full-scale siege to recapture the city, which he did in August 1521.

Failure in Florida

The first known Spanish incursion into what is now the United States was led by Juan Ponce de León in 1513. Ponce de León had led the conquest of Puerto Rico, but when he landed in Florida, he was driven off by the native people. He returned in 1521 with plans to establish a colony but was wounded in battle and died.

Curriculum Context

Students may be asked to explain the significance of the actions of certain key individuals.

Incarnation

The physical form taken by a spirit or deity.

Curriculum Context

Examining how European groups viewed the cultures they encountered in the course of their explorations helps in understanding their actions.

After de León there were other Spanish expeditions. From 1539 to 1542 Hernando de Soto led an army from Florida through Georgia and then west as far as Oklahoma, before returning down the Mississippi River to the sea. De Soto died near the end of his march, but not before he and his 600 men had fought numerous battles and plundered, tortured, and enslaved many of the native peoples they met on their journey.

Another expedition traveled north overland from Mexico about the same time. In 1540 Francisco de Coronado set out to investigate rumors of vast wealthy cities and great gold reserves. By 1541 he and his men reached as far north as Kansas, fighting several battles with the Zuni and other peoples of New Mexico and the Rio Grande Valley on the way. They found no gold and the discouraging report Coronado made on his return helped prevent further Spanish moves into this region for another half century.

This map shows the main battles that occurred between the Spanish and specific Native American peoples.

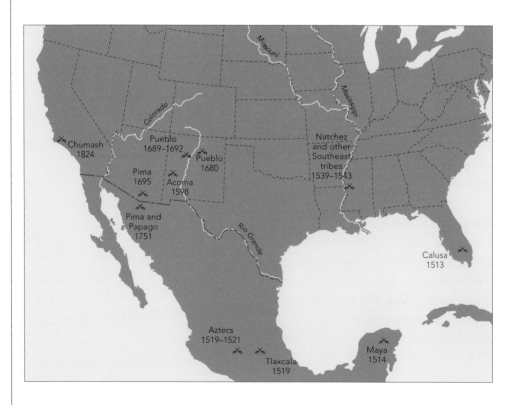

Sterilization

Sterilization—a medical procedure that ends a woman's ability to have children—was a controversial subject for Native Americans during the 1970s and 1980s. For some Native American women, not having children seemed one way to relieve economic strain. They believed it would give them independence, the freedom to seek employment, and an opportunity to gain self-reliance.

The women most likely to undergo sterilization were young reservation women. Typically they relied on state assistance, were poorly educated, and were single mothers. In reservations where up to 70 percent of the local population might be unemployed, sterilization was seen as one solution to the local economic and social problems. Even girls who had not yet reached puberty were sometimes sterilized.

Federal responsibility

Even in an age of modern health care, many Native Americans, especially those in poor rural reservation areas, did not have access to the resources of large hospitals. Instead, they were often dependent on an underfunded public health service run by poorly paid, overworked, and at times undertrained staff.

Although the hospital performing the operation had to obtain consent forms directly from the women being sterilized, these women did not always understand the forms that they were signing. It is also uncertain if the consequences of sterilization had been fully explained to them beforehand.

In the early 1990s, Native American women's action groups began working with tribal representatives and health service's to provide information and support. They began to examine ways in which unnecessary operations, such as sterilization, could be avoided.

Curriculum Context

Looking at examples of reservation life today gives students the opportunity to hypothesize about the influence of the past on the present for the Native American people.

Consent forms

A written form giving permission for something to be done.

Trail of Tears

The Trail of Tears is the name by which historians remember the removal of the Cherokee nation from their homeland. The name refers to the six months' journey the people endured between their homeland in North Carolina and the reservation in what is now Oklahoma. The Cherokee were not the only eastern nation to be taken from their lands, but their removal was the most tragic.

Like the Cherokee, most Native Americans who once lived in eastern North America no longer inhabit the lands where European colonizers first encountered their ancestors. Powerful groups once inhabited present-day Georgia, Mississippi, Louisiana, and the Carolinas. However, they were forcibly removed by the U.S. government to make room for the increasing numbers of settlers.

Following the 1830 Indian Removal Act signed by President Andrew Jackson, the peoples living east of the Mississippi River were to be relocated to the new Indian Territory, in the modern-day state of Oklahoma. The Removal Act was not welcomed by the tribes, who had lived on their lands for as long as they could remember.

The native peoples resisted their forced removal, and the Cherokee chief John Ross brought the case to the Supreme Court. Ross won his case, but President Jackson refused to accept the Supreme Court's decision. The Five Civilized Tribes—the Cherokee, Choctaw, Creek, Seminole, and Chickasaw—were ordered to leave their homelands.

Suffering of the tribes

The Choctaw nation was the first to be removed. They were forced to trek to the Indian Territory during the bitter winter of 1831–1832, the coldest winter since 1776. Nearly one-tenth of the tribe died from the journey and a cholera epidemic.

John Ross, a Cherokee chief, resisted the removal of his people and took the case to the Supreme Court...and won. Enforcing the ruling, however, was another matter.

The Cherokee put up a fierce resistance to removal from their lands in western Georgia and North Carolina. Some fled to the mountains, where their descendants still live today. Native resistance provided an excuse for the U.S. government to intervene with force.

The removal of the Cherokee began during the spring of 1838 and continued through the winter of that year. The conditions that the Cherokee had to endure were appalling. It was often freezing cold and they lacked adequate food rations. The Cherokee suffered attacks from bandits, and mud and rain made conditions worse. The army forced them to maintain a speed that many found unbearable, and the dead had to be left behind without proper burial.

About 4,000 Cherokee people are estimated to have died during the 800-mile (1,290 km) trek toward the West. This figure represents one in four of the original number who began the journey.

Curriculum Context

As part of a study of Jackson's presidency, the curriculum might ask students to describe the policy of Indian removal and its impact on Native American groups such as the Cherokee.

Treaties

Treaties are legal agreements made between opposing sides to settle disputes and define the rights and obligations of each. Treaties between Native Americans and first Europeans and later Americans usually gave white settlers access to tribal lands. In return Native Americans received guarantees that their properties and interests would be protected and that their rights to self-government would be recognized.

Curriculum Context

A careful consideration about how European nations initially saw Native Americans may give clues as to why their view later changed.

Historically, treaties were signed arrangements between sovereign, or independent, nations. This means that Native American peoples were considered independent governments. So groups that signed treaties with the United States in the 19th century, for example, can today make and enforce their own laws, set their own taxes, determine tribal membership and access to reservation areas, and control how their lands are used.

Early treaties

The first treaties signed by Native Americans were made with European powers seeking lands on which to establish their colonies and farms. At this time individual Native Americans did not own land. However, the treaties were necessary so that different European nations could legally claim particular areas and defend them against other European nations.

Native Americans did receive benefits from the treaties in the form of European trade goods to compensate for the loss of land. Native peoples were also recognized by Europeans as legal owners who were officially entitled to sell the lands they occupied.

New arrangements

When the colonies declared their independence, many old treaties were renegotiated. The first of these was made with the Delaware in 1778, but most treaties were signed during the mid-19th century. Under these new agreements treaties had to be ratified by Congress. Although native groups were still considered to be sovereign nations, the power they had to govern themselves was limited by the U.S. government. The system in Canada was only slightly different in that Canadian treaties were held in trust by the Canadian government on behalf of the British Crown.

Ratified
Agreed to; formally approved.

Injustice and removal

Many renegotiated treaties were forced on the tribes. Some were decimated by wars and new diseases brought by settlers. They had little choice but to accept treaties that gave them provisions or face starvation and extinction. Other treaties were fraudulent or deceptive.

For many nations treaties meant removal from their homelands. The Cherokee, for example, signed the New Echota Treaty in 1835, which resulted in them being moved to the Indian Territory (present-day Oklahoma) and losing their original lands.

The Cherokee had to be marched to their new lands in chains under an army guard because so many refused to go, and many died on the way. Their removal is known today as the Trail of Tears. Other peoples in the Southeast—the Creek, Chickasaw, and Choctaw—all suffered a similar fate. Those who stood up for their rights were classed as "hostiles" and were mercilessly hunted down by the U.S. Army.

Curriculum Context

Examining the impact of removal and resettlement on peoples such as the Cherokee, Creek, Chickasaw, Choctaw, and Seminole calls for an appreciation of historical perspective.

Resentment and conflict

Most of the U.S. treaties served the interests of the white communities and were intended to protect settlers and pioneers moving through or into Native American lands. Native Americans often resented these incursions because wagon trains—and later railroads—disturbed the migration routes of animals that they relied on, such as buffalo, and frightened

Incursions
Hostile raids into foreign territory.

other animals away. Some peoples, particularly on the Great Plains, resisted treaties and fought wars to keep their lands safe, but the superior military power of the United States eventually defeated them.

Fighting often broke out when the tribes realized they had been misled, when Congress failed to agree on new treaties, or when white settlers and hunters invaded tribal lands in violation of treaty agreements. In most cases the U.S. government failed in its obligations to protect Native American property.

The nature of the treaties and the aggressive attitude adopted toward native rights at the time are illustrated by the fact that the Bureau of Indian Affairs—then responsible for looking after Native American interests—

In this illustration, a native man stands between Carl Schurz, of the Interior Department, and General Philip Sheridan, of the War Department. The illustration suggests the government's ongoing struggle with the Native American situation.

was part of the War Department. It was not until 1849 that the bureau moved to the Department of the Interior and was no longer under military control.

Cultural misunderstandings

By the end of the 1850s the United States had signed 370 treaties with different tribes. Many of the treaties indicate that Native American attitudes and cultures had been misunderstood and that respect for the land—which was so vital to native people—was of little concern when that land was required for settlement. By 1870 it was becoming clear that the treaties were unrealistic, and an official end to treaty-making was declared by an act of Congress in 1871.

Protest and broken promises

More recently, the subject of treaties has been raised once more. In 1972 the issue of unkept treaty promises was raised by American Indian Movement activists. They organized a march on Washington called the "Trail of Broken Treaties Caravan" and occupied the offices of the Bureau of Indian Affairs. The intention was to raise public awareness and highlight the unresolved issues arising from broken treaty agreements.

In 1977 the American Indian Policy Review Commission was set up. It published a paper specifying that native peoples have the right to self-determination and self-government, thus ensuring them sovereignty on their lands. Nevertheless, funding to enable Native Americans to become self-sufficient has been restricted since the 1980s.

Today Native Americans argue against the loss of rights to which they believe they are legally entitled by claiming that this is a violation of the U.S. Constitution. Instead of armed conflicts a refusal to recognize treaty agreements is now argued out within the confines fo the courtroom.

Urban Life

Since World War II ended in 1945, there has been a huge increase in the number of Native Americans who choose to live in cities rather than on reservations. Before 1940 about 10 percent of Native Americans lived in cities. But during World War II, many native people joined the armed services or worked in jobs away from their reservations. In this way they broke a number of traditional ties with reservation life.

According to U.S. census counts, 13 percent of the Native American population lived in urban communities in 1950. In 1960 this figure had increased to 28 percent, but by 1970 it had risen to 45 percent—a level at which it has remained. The largest urban population of Native Americans is in Oakland, just outside San Francisco. Other large communities are in major cities such as Tulsa, Oklahoma City, New York, Chicago, and Phoenix.

The move to cities arose because of extreme poverty and low living standards on the reservations. Cities offered better jobs, higher income, and improved education, as well as government-subsidized housing and services. However, Native Americans who moved to cities found prejudice and discrimination. Many could not cope economically with competition from whites or from large and well-established minority groups.

Native identity

Native Americans also experienced difficulty in finding an identity as a group that shared common goals and common problems. Los Angeles, for example, contains about 30 Native American groups, each of which exists independently from the others. For many Native Americans urban life is a depressing experience. Many live in run-down areas with few amenities and feel isolated from the local community as well as from the traditional values of the reservations.

Government-subsidized housing

Financial assistance provided by the government to supplement housing costs.

Curriculum Context

Students should consider how issues and problems identified in the Native American past might be responsible, in part, for some of the difficulties in the present.

Combating the problem

Since the 1960s and 1970s efforts have been made to tackle the problems facing urban Native Americans. Some help has come from federally funded programs, such as those of the Department of Health, Education, and Welfare. Other projects have been sponsored by local church groups. However, the most significant effort has come from Native Americans themselves.

San Francisco has a group called United Native Americans, Minneapolis has the American Indian Movement, and American Indians United is based in Chicago. There are many other similar groups in cities throughout the country.

All the groups seek to unite Native Americans and build a sense of history and identity. Through their activities Native American issues have been brought to public attention. Today native people are developing a pride in their culture and realizing they are a powerful force, not a powerless minority.

This map shows the 17 U.S. cities with the highest Native American population.

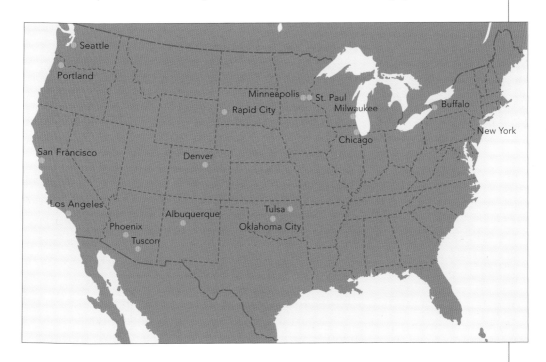

Wagon Trails

The United States grew rapidly after the American Revolution (1776-83). In 1783 it owned lands that extended only to the Mississippi and Missouri rivers, but by the middle of the 19th century it had spread across the continent to the West Coast. At the heart of this expansion were pioneer prospectors and settlers, urged on by promises of a better, more prosperous future and encouraged by government-subsidized land grants.

Transcontinental

Extending from one end of the continent to the other; going across continent.

Curriculum Context

A consideration of obstacles and difficulties to westward expansion will yield considerations both broad, such as the threat of Native Americans, and specific, such as the rough terrain.

The only way westward, before a transcontinental railroad link was completed in 1869, was by horse-drawn covered wagons. The pioneers followed old Native American trails, many of which had been enlarged and improved as military roads. Even so, travel was difficult. The terrain was often rough, slowing the progress of the heavily laden wagons. There was also a constant threat from Native Americans who resented the intrusion of settlers and wagon trains, since they frightened away many of the animals that the tribes hunted and depended on for their survival.

West to the promised land

For the pioneers, however, the West was a promised land—a country of fertile valleys in which to settle and farm or of great wealth to be obtained from gold prospecting. The wagon trails led to opportunities that could never be realized in the East. However, the trails also crossed tribal lands that had been reserved exclusively for Native American use. In 1763 the British government, which ruled the territory at that time, had drawn up the Proclamation Line, which was devised to keep colonists and Native Americans apart. But pioneers did not care that they were trespassing.

The rush for gold

The discovery of gold in California and Colorado in the middle of the 19th century greatly increased the steady stream of pioneers. One of the most famous routes used by the pioneers was the Oregon Trail, which crossed the continent from Independence, Missouri, through Nebraska, Wyoming, and Idaho to Portland, Oregon, and took six hazardous months to complete. However, danger and hardship did not deter settlers from pushing westward, lured by the promise of farmland and the chance of finding gold.

A Native American chief attempts to block settlers and their wagons from traveling through his lands.

Several other wagon routes branched off from the Oregon Trail, including the Mormon Trail to Salt Lake City in Utah. Others included the Central Overland and California trails to San Francisco. Another major trail, the Southern Overland, connected St. Louis with San Francisco via Missouri, Arkansas, Oklahoma, Texas, New Mexico, and Arizona. After gold was found in Montana in 1864, a new route, the Bozeman Trail, branched off from the Oregon Trail to head there.

Mormon

A Christian sect also known as the Church of Jesus Christ of Latter-day Saints.

Many of these old wagon trails exist today as interstate highways. They still follow the paths that Native Americans established over the centuries as the most practical routes across the continent.

War of 1812

The War of 1812, between Britain and its colony in Canada on one side and the United States on the other began in 1812 and continued until 1815. It was caused partly by a quarrel over maritime affairs but was also deliberately provoked by some U.S. leaders, who thought they saw a chance to grab territory from Canada.

The British colony of Canada was not the only target for U.S land hunger. Before the war, the United States took over more and more Native American land between the Great Lakes and the Ohio River—especially in the newly established Territory of Indiana. Native Americans fought to stop this even before 1812, which was why they chose to fight on the British side when the war started.

Attack on Prophetstown

The greatest Native American leader in the war was the Shawnee chief Tecumseh. He urged Native American groups from Florida to Canada to forget their rivalries and unite against the United States.

U.S. forces knew of Tecumseh's plans and feared, wrongly at this stage, that he was in league with the British. In the fall of 1811, Tecumseh traveled south to persuade the Creek of Georgia to join him. While he was away, U.S. forces attacked his base at Prophetstown on the Tippecanoe River in Indiana. After an indecisive battle, most Native Amererican warriors withdrew. The U.S. force burned the town.

In retaliation, Native Americans raided settlements throughout Indiana. Then in June 1812 war broke out between Britain and the United States, and Tecumseh took a large force of warriors to join the British in Canada. At one time or another warriors from at least 30 peoples fought with his army.

In the summer of 1812, Native Americans captured Forts Michilimackinac and Dearborn (Chicago), and played a major part in the British seizing Detroit. In January 1813 Tecumseh's army was largely responsible for another U.S. defeat, at Frenchtown in Michigan.

At first the British and Native Americans won most of the battles in the region, but in smaller-scale fights U.S. forces destroyed many Native American villages, forcing the inhabitants to flee. At Dearborn and other places, Native American warriors massacred many whites, but when Tecumseh was present, he stopped such atrocities.

The tide turned following the U.S. victory in the naval Battle of Lake Erie in September 1813. Tecumseh was forced to retreat along with the British. On October 5, at the Battle of the Thames, the British and Native American forces were badly beaten, and Tecumseh himself was killed.

The Shawnee chief, Tecumseh, was a major figure in the War of 1812. Here, Col. R. M. Johnson is depicted shooting Tecumseh during the Battle of the Thames.

Atrocities
Extremely cruel and brutal acts.

Water Rights

Water is vital to the survival of any community. Acess to rivers, lakes, and their resources has always been central to the relationship between Native Americans and settlers. Agricultural groups needed water to grow crops; nomadic peoples camped close to rivers that attracted large numbers of animals and also supported plant growth. The farms and ranches of European settlers were established close to the same sources of water.

Curriculum Context

Students studying Western expansion might be asked to note how relationships between Native American societies and whites changed as a result of that expansion.

Winter's Doctrine

A U.S. government document that stated that access to water had to be sufficient for the people for whom a reservation was originally created. Since the doctrine did not define how much water was considered "sufficient," some states decided that Native Americans needed very little.

Arrangements were made in early treaties between Native Americans and settlers to meet the needs of both. Generally, these arrangements worked well; but as the settler communities grew, their demands for water inevitably became greater.

Native Americans claimed rights of ancient use: that is, they believed the treaties guaranteed they would be able to use the resources their ancestors had used. But the Europeans and Americans believed the treaties should be interpreted according to their own laws and did not give Native Americans any rights to use water outside reservation areas. The Winter's Doctrine of 1908 attempted to resolve these water issues.

Dams and reservoirs

Often, little attention was paid to the water supply on reservation lands. Rivers became trickles and the levels of many lakes started to drop as their feeder rivers dried up. This decreased the amount of water available to the people and also affected the numbers of fish, waterfowl, and river and lake plant life they were able to find.

The Paiute's sacred Pyramid Lake in Nevada, for instance, was guaranteed to the tribe by treaty in 1859, but the Derby Dam—part of a government irrigation project— depleted the lake by nearly one-third. The Paiute protested against the plans and won several court cases.

However, the California–Nevada Compact of 1969 permitted water utility companies to divert even more water from Pyramid Lake to California.

The Columbia River peoples of Washington State also went to court after their rights to water, guaranteed in the Medicine Creek Treaty of 1854, were ignored. In response to their protest a court ruling in 1913 ruled that the tribes had legally ceased to exist.

Curriculum Context

In examining factors that contribute to conflicts between individuals or groups, students will recognize certain elements as being perpetual points of stress.

The situation today

Both the Paiute and Columbia River cases are typical of the way Native American concerns have been ignored. Water rights are an ongoing problem for many groups, which generally lack the resources to finance water projects of their own.

The groups rely on a commitment from federal agencies to uphold their rights. In this they are supported by international law, which specifies that access to rivers and lakes, and the fish and migratory birds they support, is an inviolable right of native peoples.

Pyramid Lake in Nevada was the source of a bitter clash between the Paiute and the U.S. government.

Wounded Knee

On December 29, 1890, approximately 250 Sioux were massacred by U.S. Army troops at Wounded Knee Creek on the Pine Ridge Sioux reservation in South Dakota. It was the last large-scale armed clash between whites and Native Americans, ending 400 years of warfare and conquest.

Little Bighorn

A battle that took place in the valley of the Little Bighorn River, Montana, in June 1876. Lieutenant Colonel George Custer and his forces suffered a crushing defeat by Sioux, Cheyenne, and Arapaho warriors.

Curriculum Context

The beliefs and behaviors of a culture shape the activities and values of that culture, as well as contribute to its experiences.

By 1889 the people of the Plains were increasingly desperate. The discovery of gold in the Black Hills and other places in the 1870s led to a huge influx of whites onto their lands. After the great victory of the Plains peoples over Custer at Little Bighorn, the U.S. Army crushed their military power and forced them onto reservations. And by the mid-1880s the buffalo that had been central to their culture had been almost wiped out.

Faced with this desperate situation, the Plains peoples sought comfort in strengthened religious belief. From 1889 the Ghost Dance movement found more and more converts among the Plains peoples. The teachings of the Ghost Dance's founder, Wovoka, were nonviolent, but prophesied that white people faced destruction. Whites found the movement threatening.

Things came to a head in late 1890, in part because of a poor harvest on the reservations that year and in part because the Bureau of Indian Affairs had cut food rations. Many Ghost Dancers gathered on the Pine Ridge Reservation. The army brought in reinforcements in November. The army's first step was to try to arrest Sitting Bull, the most respected of all the Sioux leaders. A fight broke out, and Sitting Bull was killed.

Red Cloud, a Sioux leader who lived on the Pine Ridge reservation, was friendly toward the whites and wanted to persuade the Ghost Dancers to live in peace. He asked another chief, Big Foot of the Minniconjou Sioux, to

U.S. soldiers stand amid scattered debris at Big Foot's camp after the Battle of Wounded Knee.

come to Pine Ridge and help him do this. Big Foot was a peaceable man and thought that he and his people would be safer if they joined Red Cloud, so he set off with about 120 men and 230 women and children. The army discovered that Big Foot and his band were on their way and sent patrols to intercept them.

Disaster awaits the Sioux

On December 28 part of the Seventh Cavalry, Custer's old command, caught up with Big Foot and his people. The next morning soldiers moved in to confiscate any weapons they could find. Suddenly one of the Sioux fired into the air. The soldiers panicked and began shooting at the defenseless Sioux. Within an hour, most of the Sioux were dead or dying. About 25 soldiers died with them.

The carnage shocked the whole Sioux people and largely discredited the prophecies of the Ghost Dancers, who formally surrendered to the U.S. Army on January 15, 1891. With that surrender the wars between Native Americans and whites finally came to an end.

Curriculum Context

Students should recognize the role that broken treaties, massacres, and similar occurrences played in the continual escalation of tension between Native Americans and the United States.

Carnage

The slaughter of people in a battle.

Glossary

Annexation Taking over an area in order to incorporate it into a larger territory.

Assimiliation The process of conforming to or being absorbed into a larger culture.

Chisholm Trail One of the famous cattle trails of the 1800s. Jesse Chisholm, half Scottish and half Cherokee, drove a load of buffalo hides from San Antonio, Texas, to Abilene, Kansas, for trading. The weight of his wagon left deep wheel ruts in the ground that others later followed to make the same journey.

Cholera A bacterial infection of the intestines usually contracted through the consumption of contaminated food or drinking water.

Federal Acknowledgment and Research Project An office established to review claims in regard to the government's recognition of a tribal community.

Five Civilized Tribes The Cherokee, Chickasaw, Choctaw, Creek, and Seminole were given this name by European settlers because their lives were organized in a way that reminded the colonists of their own.

French and Indian War A war (1754–1763) fought between Britain and France and their respective native allies for colonial supremacy in North America. British victory was confirmed in the Treaty of Paris in 1763.

Government-subsidized housing Financial assistance provided by the government to supplement housing costs.

Guerrilla tactics Military techniques by which small bands of warriors, often indigenous people, carry out a campaign of harassment against the enemy.

Homestead Act Passed by Congress in 1862 due to increased pressure from settlers, the act allotted unoccupied public land to U.S. citizens for a nominal fee if they could show proof of residency and land improvement over five years. Even so, the harsh conditions of the frontier made homesteading a difficult proposition.

Hudson Bay The body of water located in northeastern Canada named after the explorer Henry Hudson. The bay connects to the Atlantic Ocean on the east via the Hudson strait and the Arctic Ocean to the north. Discovery of this waterway led to the formation of the British owned Hudson's Bay Company, which greatly aided the fur trade with the Cree people.

Incarnation The physical form taken by a spirit or deity.

Indian Removal Act A federal law signed by President Andrew Jackson in 1830 authorizing the removal of Native Americans from their lands in the east and their resettlement in the west.

Jesuits A religious order of the Roman Catholic Church. It is also known as the Society of Jesus.

Little Bighorn A battle that took place in the valley of the Little Bighorn River, Montana, in June 1876. Lieutenant Colonel George Custer and his forces suffered a crushing defeat by Sioux, Cheyenne, and Arapaho warriors.

Major Crimes Act of 1885 A law that gave the United States government—instead of the individual tribal nations—authority over certain "serious" types of crime.

Migratory patterns Movements from one place to another that are often associated with the seasons, feeding, or breeding.

Militia A body of private citizens called upon for military service in times of emergency.

Mormon A Christian sect also known as the Church of Jesus Christ of Latter-day Saints.

National Congress of American Indians (NCAI) An organization founded in 1944 to secure and protect the rights of Native Americans, particularly in the courts. NCAI stresses the need for unity among tribes for the protection of their treaty and sovereign rights.

Nomadic Having no permanent home and moving from one place to another according to the seasons in search of hunting grounds, water, and grazing land.

Oral history The passing of one's culture through story-telling and memory.

Paleo-Indians Nomadic hunting people who first inhabited North America; archaeological evidence suggests these people came into existence in the late Pleistocene.

Pleistocene A period of geologic time lasting roughly from 2 million years ago to 10,000 years ago.

Political prisoners Persons who are imprisoned for involvement in political activities.

Proclamation Line An imaginary boundary line running through North America from Canada to Florida. Established in 1763, the line was supposed to separate lands meant for Native American use from those held for the colonists.

Regiment A military unit made up of several battalions of ground forces and a headquarters.

Segregation The act of keeping separate; in regard to people, segregation can call for divisions along racial, cultural, or other lines, some of which may be arbitrary.

Self-determination Freedom to control one's own direction or government.

Shaman A person regarded as having special powers to access the spirit world and an ability to use magic to heal the sick and control events.

Smallpox A contagious disease that affects humans and is marked by raised bumps on the skin. Although smallpox cases are rare—if not nonexistent—today, the illness was deadly in the early days of exploration. Smallpox brought by explorers and settlers sometimes wiped out most of a native settlement.

Sovereignty Complete independence to self-govern without external influence or control.

Subsidies Grants of money as a means of assistance. Often this money is given by the government to an individual, but it can also be granted from one body to another.

Vision Quest A rite of passage in many Native American groups, in which young individuals go alone to an isolated place to seek protection from the spirits.

Winter's Doctrine A U.S. government document that stated that access to water had to be sufficient for the people for whom a reservation was originally created. Since the doctrine did not define how much water was considered "sufficient," some states decided that Native Americans needed very little.

Further Research

BOOKS

Anderson, Fred. *The War That Made America: A Short History of the French and Indian War*. Penguin, 2006.

Bowes, John P. *The Trail of Tears: Removal in the South*. Chelsea House Publications, 2007.

Brown, Dee. *Bury My Heart at Wounded Knee: An Indian History of the American West*. Holt Paperbacks, 2007.

Child, Brenda J. *Boarding School Seasons, American Indian Families 1900–1940*. University of Nebraska Press, 2000.

Deloria, Vine, and David E. Wilkins. *Tribes, Treaties, and Constitutional Tribulations*. University of Texas Press, 2000.

Dowd, Gregory Evans. War *Under Heaven: Pontiac, the Indian Nations, and the British Empire*. Johns Hopkins University Press, 2004.

Jackson, Helen Hunt. *A Century of Dishonor: the Classic Exposé of the Plight of the Native Americans*. Dover Publications, 2003.

Johansen, Bruce E. *The Native Peoples of North America: A History*. Rutgers University Press, 2006.

Nabokov, Peter. *Native American Testimony*. Penguin, 1999.

Nerburn, Kent. *Chief Joseph & the Flight of the Nez Perce: The Untold Story of an American Tragedy*. HarperOne, 2006.

Ostler, Jeffrey. *The Plains Sioux and U.S. Colonialism from Lewis and Clark to Wounded Knee*. Cambridge University Press, 2004.

Patent, Dorothy Hinshaw. *The Buffalo and the Indians: A Shared Destiny*. Clarion Books, 2006.

Pritzker, Barry M., ed. *A Native American Encyclopedia: History, Culture, & Peoples*. Oxford University Press, USA, 2000.

Roberts, David. *Once They Moved Like the Wind: Cochise, Geronimo, and the Apache Wars*. Touchstone, 2005.

Sandos, James A. *Converting California: Indians and Franciscans in the Missions*. Yale University Press, 2008.

Smith, Paul Chaat, and Robert Allen Warrior. *Like a Hurricane: The Indian Movement from Alcatraz to Wounded Knee*. New Press, 1997.

Utley, Robert M., and Wilcomb E. Washburn. *Indian Wars*. Mariner Books, 2002.

West, Elliott. *The Contested Plains: Indians, Goldseekers, and the Rush to Colorado*. University Press of Kansas, 2000.

Yenne, Bill. *Indian Wars: The Campaign for the American West*. Westholme Publishing, 2008.

INTERNET RESOURCES

American Indian Tribal/Nation Home Pages. A University of Oklahoma website, with links to the home pages of Native American peoples.
www.law.ou.edu/native/ainations.shtml

The Canadian Encyclopedia. Articles on the fur trade, the Métis, the Riel rebellions, and each of Canada's First Peoples.
www.thecanadianencyclopedia.com

National Museum of the American Indian. The Smithsonian Institution's National Museum of the American Indian website. The site provides information about the museum's collections as well as educational resources for students about the history and culture of Native Americans.
www.nmai.si.edu/

Native American History. Site from the University of Washington with links to information on all aspects of Native American history.
www.lib.washington.edu/subject/history/tm/native.html

NativeAmericans.com. A comprehensive site with information and links about all aspects of Native American culture and history, including online biographies, extensive bibliographies, and information about the history and culture of Native American groups.
www.nativeamericans.com

Native Americans Documents Project. Provides access to documents relating to Native American history, including federal Indian policy and the Dawes General Allotment Act.
www2.csusm.edu/nadp/

NativeWeb. A website with links to all aspects of Native American studies including law and legal issues, and native activism.
www.nativeweb.org/

Seminole History. Information on the history of the Seminole people of Florida, including Osceola and the Seminole Wars, from the Florida Department of State.
www.flheritage.com/facts/history/seminole/

Smithsonian: American Indian History and Culture. A Smithsonian Institution website, with information about all aspects of Native American history and culture.
www.si.edu/Encyclopedia_SI/History_and_Culture/AmericanIndian_History.htm

Index

Tewa 66, 67
Three Warriors (movie, 1977) 61
Tiguex 68
Tlingit 56, 57, 80
Tonkawa 42
Trail of Broken Treaties Caravan 64, 95
Trail of Tears 90–91, 93
treaties 6, 14, 22–23, 47, 64, 72, 73, 75, 81, 86, 92–95, 102, 103
  Adams–Onís 82
  Medicine Creek 102
  New Echota 47, 93
  Paris 35
  Paynes Landing 82
  Utrecht 39
tribal governments 19, 32, 49, 50, 51, 76
Tusayan 68

Ulzana's Raid (movie, 1972) 60
United Native Americans 97
urban life 96–97

Vargas, Diego de 67
Vision Quest 25

Waco 42
wagon trails 98–99, *99*, 93–94
  Bozeman Trail 99
  California Trail 99
  Central Overland Trail 99
  Mormon Trail 99
  Oregon Trail 99
  Southern Overland Trail 99
Wampanoag 48, 72
War of 1812 82, 100–101, *101*
Washington, George 34
water rights 23, 102–103

Wea 43
Western Trail *21*
Western Union (movie, 1941) 60
Wheeler–Howard Act 7
Wichita 43, 68
Winnebago 27
Winter's Doctrine 102
Wounded Knee, battle of 37, 104–105, *105*
Wounded Knee II 64, 65
Wovoka (Paiute shaman) 36, 37, 57, 104
Wratten, George 45
Wyandot 43

Yakima 41, *41*, 77

Zambos 53
Zuni 68, 88